THE **FIELD GUIDE** TO
PEPPERS

THE FIELD GUIDE TO
PEPPERS

Dave DeWitt & Janie Lamson

TIMBER PRESS
PORTLAND, OREGON

All photos by Janie Lamson except those on pages 20, 212, 226, and 280 by Dave
DeWitt, and on page 290 by Mircea Dobre. Title page illustration by Walther
Müller and Carl Friedrich (C. F.) Schmidt from *Köhler's Medizinal-Pflanzen Atlas*,
1887. Gera, Germany. Biodiversity Heritage Library.

The Haseltine Building
133 S.W. Second Avenue, Suite 450
Portland, Oregon 97204–3527
timberpress.com

Printed in China

Cover design by Briar Levit
Book design by Skye McNeill

Library of Congress Cataloging-in-Publication Data

DeWitt, Dave, author.
    The field guide to peppers / Dave DeWitt and Janie Lamson.—First edition.
      pages cm
    Includes index.
    ISBN 978-1-60469-588-5
    1. Peppers—Identification. I. Lamson, Janie, author. II. Title.
    QK495.S7D478 2016
    583'.952—dc23
                                                          2015019431

A catalog record for this book is also available from the British Library.

Contents

Preface

My interest in chile peppers is directly related to a goal I set in 1975, after moving from Richmond, VA, to Albuquerque, NM, to start my writing career. The move led to a radical change in my garden and in my diet as I began to grow and eat chile peppers on a regular basis, especially the New Mexican varieties. Within a year, I had totally adapted to a new lifestyle and was hooked on my new state's official "vegetable," but I wanted to learn more about capsicums and share that information with others, so that's just what I did.

I began my career by writing magazine and newspaper articles, often about travel and food in New Mexico, and as I traveled around the state, I stopped at libraries and asked the librarians if they had a file on chile peppers; if they did, I asked to make a copy of it. More often than not they had one and then so did I. That was a modest beginning for a 40-year project that involved launching two magazines, founding a national trade show, building a huge website, and authoring or co-authoring almost 40 books on chile peppers and spicy foods. I had found my niche, and I've loved every moment of it. The media even took to calling me the "Pope of Peppers."

I also had the opportunity to travel the world and experience chile peppers as they are used in a variety of world cuisines, from wine made solely from chiles in Australia to the scorching vindaloo in Mumbai and Nando's chicken in South Africa that's spiced with peri-peri peppers. I've fallen for every cuisine I've tasted, but I'm always remained loyal to the New Mexican cuisine that got me started with this obsession.

This book is the next step in organizing and presenting that knowledge. Taking into account the nomenclature, identification, and growth habits of hundreds of varieties of the most popular chiles grown in the United States, it has been a massive challenge. My first attempt at doing this was in 1996, when Paul W. Bosland and I wrote *Peppers of the World: An Identification*

Guide. For that book we grew out hundreds of varieties of peppers from the USDA seed banks, photographed them, and organized them into a fairly useful guide with one significant drawback: most of the varieties had a USDA number but no cultivar name.

Fortunately for chileheads, there was another person out there doing the hands-on, basic research necessary for a book like this: Janie Lamson of Cross Country Nurseries in New Jersey. It was Janie and her staff who germinated and grew out all of the most popular garden peppers, all the while assembling the data on plant and pod sizes, colors, and growing habits. All of the 400 varieties selected for this book *do* have names, and Janie offers the live plants that you can purchase for your own garden from her nursery.

Dave DeWitt, the Pope of Peppers

My love of plants began when I was a child. From playing in my mother's beautiful flower gardens to hiking deep into the woods with my father, I just loved the outdoors and all the beautiful plants that I found there. Working with and being surrounded by nature was first my hobby and then my vocation.

When my family relocated in 1984, I began building a small nursery on a 6-acre field in the front of the property. Within a year, Cross Country Nurseries was born, growing perennials, ornamental grasses, and ferns, mostly for the landscape trade. In 1993, we grew out nine varieties of chiles. They were easy to grow and I was intrigued by the beautiful fruits the plants produced. In 1994, while waiting in long lines to get into an exhibit about peppers at the Philadelphia Flower Show, I overheard many people passionately talking about peppers. "Hmmm," I thought. "There may be something to these peppers."

For fun, more chile varieties were added each year, reaching 84 varieties by 1996, which were sold alongside the perennials. Then the phone calls started. "I hear you have chile plants. Do you ship?" We didn't, and knew that the hardest part of expansion would be designing a shipping container. After many prototypes, we developed a solution that got plants to their destination in perfect condition, even after being sent upside down! In 1997, we began shipping 101 varieties of hot chile plants by mail order. Happy customers began calling me the "Chile Goddess."

My first digital camera arrived in 1998, and one of the first photos taken was of the chile variety 'Aurora'. I was hooked. The wide diversity of colors, shapes, and sizes fascinated me, and I began photographing all of the varieties. In 1999, my first photos appeared on our website, ChilePlants.com, which now also included sweet peppers. In 2000, we discontinued perennials to instead focus solely on peppers. By 2005, we were also shipping tomato plants and in 2008, eggplants.

ChilePlants.com, working out of 12 greenhouses, currently offers 500 varieties of chiles and sweet pepper plants, 180 varieties of tomatoes, and 65 eggplant varieties. We grow from seeds both purchased commercially and saved on site. We are especially interested in keeping strains from becoming extinct, and love reuniting folks with long-lost favorites. Each year we trial new varieties, looking for strong growers and good producers. Plants are grown on a diet of fish emulsion and seaweed, with beneficial insects for pest control. From April through mid-June, we fill a tractor-trailer weekly with plant orders shipped throughout the United States, and our walk-in nursery is open from mid-April through May. In September, we offer fresh chiles by mail order—freshly picked, delicious fruits shipped right to the customers' doors.

Peppers continue to fascinate me, and after working with them for so many years I have come to know them well. A day in the fields with my camera is a day crouching among pepper plants, getting up close and personal, trying to capture their beautiful essence. I hope that my passion for peppers will come across through this guide and will inspire you on your own journey to explore and discover these amazing fruits.

Janie Lamson, the Chile Goddess

A Brief Guide to Growing

Because there is such a wide number of pepper varieties available to the home gardener, choosing the best varieties for your garden is easy. Seed companies and state college experiment stations devote tremendous effort to the development of disease-resistant, highly productive varieties that are tailor-made for different climactic conditions. Some of these new varieties may be better than the ones gardeners traditionally grow.

In our experience, you can grow almost all varieties anywhere, but some will produce better than others. Gardeners often purchase pepper seed without knowing if the variety is adapted to local climactic conditions. For example, the New Mexican varieties grow well in the hot, dry Southwest but may not produce as well in more moderate northern regions (though we grow them without much trouble in New Jersey). Conversely, bells and habaneros do not grow as well in the Southwest as they do in other regions.

The best approach is to simply learn from experience. To decide which varieties to plant, consult your gardening neighbors, a local gardening club, or the county agricultural or extension agent. When reading the variety description on the seed packet or in the catalog, look for the qualities that are most important for success, such as growing period, yield, disease resistance, and recommendations for climactic zones. Some varieties are best suited for pickling, some for drying, some for fresh use, and some for processing and freezing.

The early or late maturity of a variety is also a very important consideration. At high altitudes or in cool climates, both with short growing seasons, the pepper variety must be able to mature and set fruit rapidly. Early-maturing varieties are valuable to the cool-climate gardener who might not be able to mature the late cultivars at all because of their long season requirements, or to the hot-climate gardener who wants an early harvest.

Many new varieties of peppers are hybrids that are superior to the older variety of the same or similar name. Hybrid varieties often have resistance to one or more diseases, grow rapidly, and produce more uniform pods than the older variety. Hybrids may cost more, but for most gardeners the disease resistance alone is worth the price. This fact is especially true for organic gardeners who eschew pesticides. Keep in mind that hybrids do not reproduce true to type because they are only second-generation crosses, so saving seed from hybrid varieties is not worth the effort.

After choosing the best varieties for your garden, along with any accompanying plants, your next step is to plan. There are many factors to take into consideration when designing your garden: site, soil type, rainfall, method of irrigation, mature height of various plants, structural support for plants, and access to the garden for weeding and harvesting.

For your chile garden, these are the basic designs:

Ridges and furrows
Perhaps the most familiar of all garden designs, this type has alternating ridges (or hills) and furrows (or trenches). The plants grow along the ridges and are irrigated from the furrows.

Flat beds
This garden design is perhaps the simplest to construct. After soil preparation, the site is surrounded by a berm (raised soil) that will hold water during flood irrigating or after rainfall.

Raised beds
Used primarily for good drainage, this above-ground system uses bricks, blocks, logs, or wood planks to contain the garden above the usual soil level.

Sunken beds
This design, used by the ancient Egyptians, is the opposite of

ridges and furrows. The plants are placed in the furrows, where they are protected from high winds until they are well established.

Modified irrigated beds

After years of growing peppers in small plots in the Southwest, we have developed a system that works well because it allows us to grow peppers with most of the other vegetables and herbs in the garden. Chile plots are surrounded on three or four sides by irrigation ditches to provide maximum moisture in New Mexico's extremely dry climate.

Containers

Chile gardeners can also grow plants in large pots (with a minimum size of 5 gallons, though 10- to 15-gallon pots are preferred), whiskey barrel halves, or even well-drained trash cans. The rule of thumb is that the larger the pod, the larger the pot. Small fruiting varieties like piquíns can even be grown in a small 1-gallon pot, but production will be reduced. People who live in apartments and townhouses without gardens can grow peppers and other plants on their balconies, patios, or even in a closet under lights. The peppers can be moved around easily, transforming the peppers from patio plants into ornamental houseplants.

The Ideal Pepper Soil

It is unlikely that the perfect soil for growing peppers exists in its natural state anywhere in the country, so some soil treatment will undoubtedly be necessary. Generally speaking, the best pepper-growing soil has the following characteristics: a warm, full-sun location; well-drained loam or sandy loam high in organic material but with moderate fertility; a herbicide-free environment; little or no alkali; and a pH registering from 6.0–8.0 (ideally 6.7–7.3). It is best to rotate your garden crops so that you don't deplete the soil of the nutrition needed for good production, but we know this is not always possible. Be sure to add lots of organic matter—such as manure, compost, dried leaves, or peat—to your soil every year to keep it fresh and full of nutrition.

Start your pepper seeds in a shallow tray or pot about six to ten weeks before it's time to transplant seedlings to the garden—just like commercial greenhouses do. We use a peat-based growing medium and lightly cover seeds a quarter-inch deep, and then moisten. The trays or pots are set in trays on top of red rubber propogation mats to keep soil temperatures at 80–90°F during the day and 70–75°F at night. The warmth of the soil can radically affect the germination percentage of most chile varieties. A recent comparison of germination techniques for wild chiltepín seeds revealed that heating the soil increased germination percentages from 10 to 80 percent.

Many varieties of pepper seeds would benefit from using saltpetre (potassium nitrate). Saltpetre softens the seedcoat and is wonderful for difficult-to-germinate pepper varities such as habaneros, chiltepíns, and rocotos, as well as for older seed. Mix a teaspoon per quart of warm water. Soak seed in a coffee filter in a plastic cup for 24–48 hours and then sow immediately.

A humidity dome or sheet of plastic keeps soil temperatures and moisture levels consistent and quickens the process of germination. Avoid letting the soil become saturated. Take off the cover or plastic for at least 10 minutes every day. Allow the soil surface to dry between waterings, but do not allow the soil to completely dry out.

The seedlings should be grown in very bright light or full sun so they do not become "leggy" and topple over. If growing under lights, keep the lights on for 16 hours a day (and off for 8). Some leggy seedlings may be pinched back to make a bushier plant. Keep the seedlings moist but not wet; overwatering will cause stem rot. We use only organic fertilizers on our plants, starting with a liquid seaweed solution at sowing. Seaweed or kelp is like a multivitamin for plants, keeping them healthy and free from stress, as well being high in potassium for good root development. After the plants have put out their second set of true leaves (their third set of leaves total), we add liquid fish emulsion to the seaweed solution. We apply at half strength to start, gradually increasing concentration as the plants grow. This is also a good time to pot up into a slightly larger pot to grow on. We have found that potting up into only slightly larger pots at first (as opposed to immediately moving on to larger pots) gets the plants to grow larger much more quickly. Once plants are in their final pot or garden spot we topdress them with a granular organic fertilizer, which provides strong growth and readies them for good production. When growing seedlings in the house, remember that cats love to graze on tender young plants—harmless for your cats, but this will destroy the plants.

Peppers should be set out in the garden two to three weeks after your expected last frost, when night temperatures are consistently above 55°F and the temperature of the garden soil 4 inches below the surface reaches 65°F. One week before transplanting, the seedlings should be "hardened off" by placing the trays outside for a few hours each day when the weather is warm and sunny, increasing the time a little more each day until the plants can remain in full sun for most of the day—it is important not to rush this part. Constant movement of the seedlings from light breezes will strengthen the stems and prepare the plants for the rigors of the garden.

If the garden plot is to be irrigated, use a shovel to make rows and furrows and then set the chile pepper plants 2 feet apart. It is possible to cram more plants into the garden, or to reduce the square footage used, but this size and spacing works best for us because it enables us to harvest the pods without stomping on the plants. Some gardeners place the peppers as close as a foot apart so the plants will shade each other and protect the fruit from sunburn. If necessary, protect young plants from freak frosts by covering them with sheets or thin blankets supported on a frame of posts or branches.

After transplanting your peppers, the garden should be thoroughly mulched. Mulch holds in moisture and keeps heat out, which makes for cool and moist roots and a much happier plant. We like to use a thick 5-inch layer of a grass-type mulch like straw or hay. To keep weed seeds in the mulch from germinating, put several layers of newspaper down first with the straw or hay on top. Wood chips or wood mulch is not recommended as they steal nitrogen from the plants as the wood breaks down. If you must use wood mulch, extra nitrogen fertilizer will be needed, some for the plants and some for the wood mulch.

Peppers need moist roots, but overwatering is the biggest mistake of the home gardener. The best time to check your plants to see if they need water is in the morning, and not during the heat of day or at night. To check, lift the mulch around the plant, dig down 5–6 inches, and feel the soil. If it is dry, then you'll need to water. If moist, leave it be. Do not keep the soil saturated, and be sure to water the ground and not the foliage. Never water everyday. Keep in mind that some of the wilting that you see in the hot summer sun is normal and is not an indication of any moisture needs.

A well-balanced fertilizer encourages strong growth but high-nitrogen fertilizers should be discontinued after plants are full sized and beginning to flower. Phosphorous encourages flower and fruit production. In order to set fruit, the plants require daytime temperatures between 65° and 80°F and night temperatures above 55°F. Flowering decreases during the hottest months of the summer, and, in fact, extremely hot or dry conditions will result in the blossoms dropping off the plant. However, in the early fall, flowering picks up again but in cooler northern regions fall blooms are unlikely to yield fruit. In most locations, the first hard frost will kill the plants and may damage the fruits, so pick all remaining fruits before frost is expected.

Diseases and pests can attack pepper plants, particularly when they're in the seedling stage. Be on the lookout for aphids, white fly, and spider mites in the greenhouse. Peppers in the garden are sometimes infected with phytophthora or wilt disease, which is promoted by overly wet soil. In all cases, remove all diseased plants and destroy them. In the garden, pepper plants and pods can be assaulted by a large number of insect pests, including aphids, beetles, borers, bugs, flies, hoppers, miners, mites, scales, and worms. Fortunately, these attacks are usually not fatal for the plants as long as they are being fertilized properly. Here again seaweed is a great addition to your fertilizing solution, as it raises the brix or sugar level of the leaf, which is undesirable to sucking or rasping insects. It also helps the plant get over the stresses of insect assault or other less than perfect environmental conditions. The viruses, especially curly top, are fatal and infected plants should be destroyed.

We are often asked if cultivation techniques can alter the amount of capsaicin in the pods and make the peppers hotter or milder. The amount of capsaicin in chiles is genetically fixed, which means that the plants will breed true to their heat levels under ideal conditions. However, stress on the plants in the form of heat or drought can dramatically increase the heat levels, according to researchers at New Mexico State University. Cool and wet conditions can make pods milder.

For harvesting, we recommend the staggered harvesting technique, which means that the chiles in the garden can be used all season long. Usually the first peppers available are those which are small and used green in fresh salsas—the serranos, jalapeños, and the young green pods of other varieties such as habaneros. Some peppers, especially varieties such as the poblanos and the Anaheim or New Mex types such as 'Big Jim' and 'Española Improved' can be eaten or processed as soon as they are about 4 inches long, or they can be allowed to turn red before picking and drying. However, there are a few varieties that are generally used only in their dried state, such as cayenne and santaka chiles.

It is important to continue harvesting the ripe pods as they mature. If the pods are allowed to remain on the plant, few new ones will form, whereas if the pods are continuously harvested, the plants will produce great numbers of pods. The best time to pick peppers for drying is when they first start to turn red or their final color. This picking will stimulate the plant into further production and the harvested peppers can be strung to dry and will turn bright red. When harvesting, it is best to cut the peppers off the plants with a knife or scissors because brittle branches will often break before the stem of the pepper pod will.

More detailed information on chile gardening can be found in *The Complete Chile Pepper Book*, by Dave DeWitt and Paul W. Bosland.

How to Use This Book

The aim of this book is twofold: to identify unfamiliar pepper varieties that you might come across and to assist in the selection of peppers for your garden. We used a simple selection process to select the varieties that appear in the book: we've included the 400 best-selling varieties sold by Cross Country Nurseries at ChilePlants.com (Janie's company). You'll likely only grow a few of the varieties covered here, but at least you can see and compare, with a few glances, the choices of, say, the most popular jalapeño varieties.

Since there are five domesticated species of peppers, the book is divided into five sections: *Capsicum annuum, C. baccatum, C. chinense, C. frutescens,* and *C. pubescens. Capsicum annuum* is such a large and diverse species that it is further divided into pod types (varieties with similar pod shapes).

The following information categories are included in each variety description:

CULTIVAR NAME

Take all names with a grain of salt, because they are often arbitrary, generic, unscientific, and inaccurate. And note that sometimes names are reversed, as in 'Chocolate Cherry' or 'Cherry Chocolate'.

Chile nomenclature can be confusing—for example, *Capsicum chinense* describes a plant of Western Hemisphere origin—and often vague at best, like 'Chile Verde', which means green chile. We have endeavored to give accurate alternative names for the varieties included.

ORIGIN

This tells you where the variety first appeared in human agriculture, or if a hybrid, where it was developed. Sometimes we make our best guess based on our knowledge and experience of decades of working with chile peppers.

PODS

We include the length and width for each plant, based on the average of Janie's plants at Cross Country Nurseries over time, along with some notes on appearance and color.

PLANT HEIGHT

Again, our measurements are based on the average of Janie's plants (grown in New Jersey) over time. As Janie puts it, "When we trial a variety, we take down measurements. If we continue with that variety we will compare those measurements with our original trial data, and make changes and adjustments as necessary. We have been doing this since we first started growing peppers in 1993."

HARVEST

We are frequently asked about the best time to actually pick peppers off the plant, and we encourage readers to pick at all stages of the maturation process and try them. Some varieties are better when a bit immature and not fully colored. Varities to be used for pickling should be picked when young in order to keep some crunch to the pod. Usually the heat level is lower when pods are immature. Varieties to be dried should be allowed to ripen before picking. We also offer our typical schedules for pepper harvesting, in our experience. The time ranges we include here are set for Cross Country Nurseries, 199 Kingwood-Locktown Road, Stockton, New Jersey 08559, latitude and longitude 40.43° N, 74.98° W, USDA zone 6B. That said, Janie believes that her nursery is more zone 5 than zone 6 because of its microclimate features. Plants are planted out in the field in early June with frost typically arriving early to mid-October.

HEAT LEVEL

Heat levels are determined through a combination of tests using high-performance liquid chromatography, tasting reports from individuals, and our own personal experience, with data collected for more than a decade. The typical chile plant or seed buyer uses common terms like the ones here when requesting peppers.

sweet = nonpungent

mild = less than 2500 SHUs (Scoville Heat Units)

medium = 2500–10,000 SHU

hot = 10,000–50,000 SHU

very hot = 50,000–350,000 SHU

extremely hot = 350,000–900,000 SHU

super hot = 900,000 or more SHU

COMMENTS

These include growing observations, culinary use, interesting factoids, and notes on chile pepper nomenclature.

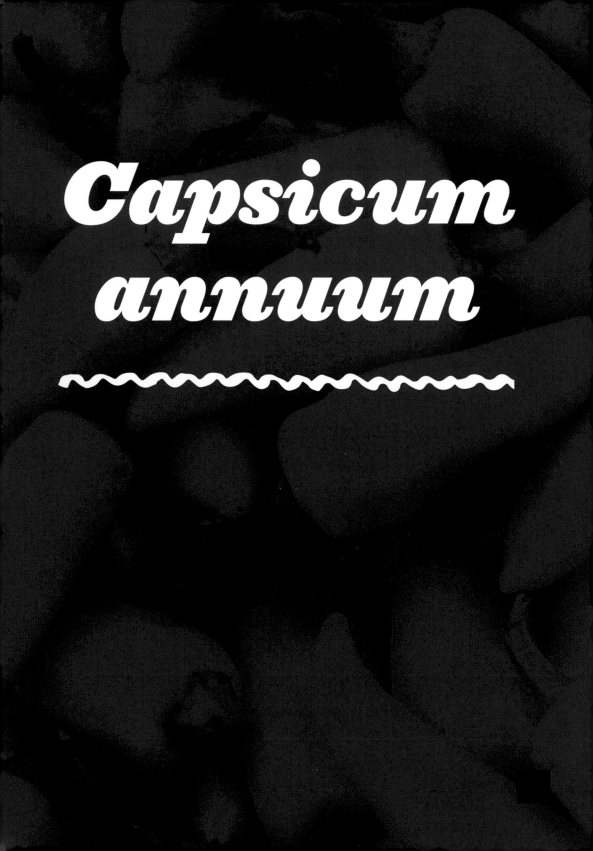

Capsicum annuum

〜〜〜〜〜〜〜〜〜〜〜〜〜〜〜〜〜〜〜〜

Annum means annual, which is an incorrect designation, as peppers are perennials. Chile peppers are grown as annuals in Europe, where most of the nomenclature was developed, and this fact probably caused the inaccurate species name.

This species includes most of the commonest varieties, such as New Mexican, jalapeño, bell, and wax.

The most likely ancestor of the common *C. annuum* varieties grown in the garden today is the wild chiltepín. Botanists believe that these wild chiles are the closest surviving species to the earliest forms of chiles that developed in Bolivia and southern Brazil, long before humankind arrived in the New World. The wild chiles spread all over South and Central America thanks to birds who loved the vitamin A–loaded bright red pods and deposited their undigested seeds as a perfect natural fertilizer. The birds moved the wild chiltepíns up to what is now the US border millennia before the domesticated varieties arrived. In fact, some botanists believe that chiltepíns or their variants (piquíns) have the widest distribution of any Western Hemisphere chile variety, ranging from throughout South America from Peru north to the Caribbean, Florida, Louisiana, then to Texas, and on to southern Arizona.

Further south, Aztec plant breeders had already developed dozens of *C. annuum* varieties by the time the Spanish arrived in Mexico. According to historian Bernardino de Sahagún, who lived in Mexico in 1529, "hot green peppers, smoked peppers, water peppers, tree peppers, beetle peppers, and sharp-pointed red peppers" existed. Undoubtedly, these peppers were the precursors to the large number of *C. annuum* varieties found in Mexico today. Christopher Columbus took *C. annuum* seeds back to the Old World, and they were planted extensively in the Portuguese and Spanish colonies in Africa, India, and Asia, resulting in even more diversification of the species.

Capsicum annuum is the most extensively cultivated species in the world, both commercially and in home gardens. It is the principal species grown in Hungary, India, Mexico, China, Korea, and the East Indies. Because the varieties cross-pollinate so easily, probably thousands of different types exist around the world. Each has a common name, making identification difficult. In Mexico, for example, more than 200 common names for peppers are used—but only about 15 *C. annuum* pod types are cultivated commercially.

Capsicum annuum used to be divided into just two categories, sweet (or mild) peppers and hot (or chile) peppers. However, modern plant breeding has removed that distinction because hot bell varieties and nonpungent jalapeño and New Mexican varieties have been bred. Now the vast *C. annuum* species is organized according to the shape and position of the pods. As is to be expected in a species with so many cultivated and uncultivated varieties, some overlap will occur. For example, certain varieties in the piquín pod type are bred only for their vibrant colors, so they have been placed in the ornamental pod type.

Ancho

The name *ancho* means "wide" or "broad," an allusion to the flat, heart-shaped pods in the dried form. The fresh pod is known as a poblano, meaning "of the people." In Mexico and the United States, it is a large, broad, mild chile with a raisiny aroma and flavor. Confusingly, anchos are called *pasillas* in Morelia, Michoacán, and *chile joto* in Aguascalientes, while poblanos are known as *pasillas* in some northern states of Mexico and in California.

Anchos are multistemmed and semi-erect, semi-woody, and about 24–36 inches high. The leaves are dark green and shiny. The corollas are off-white and appear at every node. The flowering period begins 50 days after transplanting and continues until the first frost. The pods are pendant, vary between 3–6 inches long, and are 2–3 inches wide. They are conical or truncated and have indented shoulders. Immature pods are dark green, maturing to either red or brown. The dried pods are a very dark reddish brown, nearly black. They are fairly mild, ranging from 1000 to 1500 SHUs. The dried pods are more pungent than the fresh.

These varieties are some of the most popular peppers grown in Mexico, where about 37,000 acres of them are under cultivation. They grow well in the United States but only about 150 acres are planted. Growers in the eastern United States (in Wharton, New Jersey) reported that their plants topped 4 feet and needed to be staked to keep from toppling over. They produced well but the pods never matured to the red stage before the end of the growing season. The usual growing period is 70 to 90 days after transplanting.

Fresh poblanos are roasted and peeled, then preserved by canning or freezing. They are often stuffed to make chiles rellenos. The dried pods can be stored in airtight containers for months, or they can be ground into a powder. Anchos, along with chilhuacles, a related variety, are commonly used in mole sauces.

Ancho 101

Capsicum annuum 'Ancho 101'

ORIGIN Mexico

PODS 3–4 in. long, 2–3 in. wide; pendant, dark green to red

PLANT HEIGHT 30–36 in.

HARVEST Midseason, 70–80 days after transplanting

HEAT LEVEL Mild

One of the original varieties bred in Mexico, 'Ancho 101' is one of the most commonly grown ancho varities, with slightly smaller pods.

Ancho 211 Hybrid

Capsicum annuum 'Ancho 211 Hybrid'

ORIGIN United States

PODS 4–5 in. long, 2–2.5 in. wide; pendant, dark green to red

PLANT HEIGHT 24–30 in.

HARVEST Midseason, 70–80 days after transplanting

HEAT LEVEL Medium

A newer hybrid with hotter pods, this is a large stuffing pepper, but it's also dried and used in mole powders and sauces.

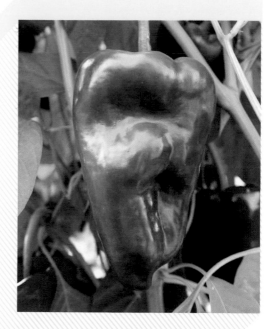

Ancho Gigantia

Capsicum annuum 'Ancho Gigantia'

ORIGIN Mexico

PODS 4–6 in. long, 2.5–3 in. wide; pendant, dark green to red

PLANT HEIGHT 36–42 in.

HARVEST Midseason, 70–80 days after transplanting

HEAT LEVEL Mild

Sometimes spelled 'Ancho Gigantea'. These large pods are perfect for making stuffed chiles. Roast them and peel them first.

Ancho L

Capsicum annuum 'Ancho L'

ORIGIN Mexico

PODS 4–6 in. long, 2.5–3 in. wide; pendant, dark green to brown

PLANT HEIGHT 36–42 in.

HARVEST Midseason, 70–80 days after transplanting

HEAT LEVEL Mild

A brown pod, with good production. Good for stuffing, or dried into a powder for mole sauce.

Ancho Large Mexican

Capsicum annuum 'Ancho Large Mexican'

ORIGIN Mexico

PODS 4–5 in. long, 2–3 in. wide; pendant, dark green to red

PLANT HEIGHT 30–36 in.

HARVEST Midseason, 70–80 days after transplanting

HEAT LEVEL Mild

These pods have large cavities that are great for stuffing. Also dried for powder.

Ancho Mulato

Capsicum annuum 'Ancho Mulato'

ORIGIN Mexico (Jalisco, Guanajuato, and Puebla)

PODS 3–5 in. long, 2–2.5 in. wide; pendant, dark green to brown

PLANT HEIGHT 36–42 in.

HARVEST Midseason, 70–80 days after transplanting

HEAT LEVEL Mild

A type of dried poblano chile in Mexico that has very dark brown, almost black, pods.

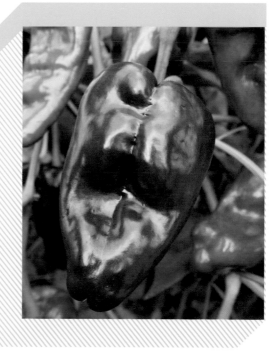

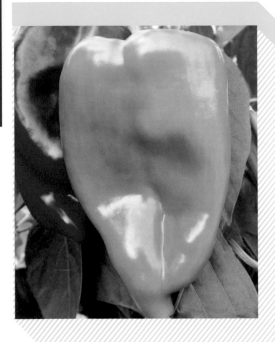

Ancho Ranchero Hybrid

Capsicum annuum **'Ancho Ranchero Hybrid'**

ORIGIN United States

PODS 4–5 in. long, 2.5–3.5 in. wide; pendant, green to red

PLANT HEIGHT 30–36 in.

HARVEST Midseason, 70–80 days after transplanting

HEAT LEVEL Mild

The huge pods are the size of bells on tall, sturdy plants.

Ancho San Luis

Capsicum annuum **'Ancho San Luis'**

ORIGIN Mexico

PODS 4–6 in. long, 2.5–3 in. wide; pendant, dark green to red

PLANT HEIGHT 36–42 in.

HARVEST Midseason, 70–80 days after transplanting

HEAT LEVEL Mild

This ancho has uniform, heart-shaped peppers and is prolific.

Ancho San Martin Hybrid

Capsicum annuum **'Ancho San Martin Hybrid'**

ORIGIN United States

PODS 4–6 in. long, 2.5–3.5 in. wide; pendant, green to red

PLANT HEIGHT 36–42 in.

HARVEST Midseason, 70–80 days after transplanting

HEAT LEVEL Mild

Large size and prolific production are what make this ancho pepper distinctive.

Chilhuacle Amarillo

Capsicum annuum **'Chilhuacle Amarillo'**

ORIGIN Mexico (Oaxaca)

PODS 3–3.5 in. long, 1–1.25 in. wide; pendant, green to yellow orange

PLANT HEIGHT 18–24 in.

HARVEST Midseason, 70–80 days after transplanting

HEAT LEVEL Medium

Sometimes spelled 'Chilguacle Amarillo'. In Mexico, this Oaxacan chile is primarily used in mole sauces. Some sources say that it is a regional variety of guajillo, but others say it more closely resembles a small, thin poblano.

Chilhuacle Negro

Capsicum annuum 'Chilhuacle Negro'

ORIGIN Mexico (Oaxaca)

PODS 3–4 in. long, 2.5–3.5 in. wide; pendant, velvety green to brown

PLANT HEIGHT 18–24 in.

HARVEST Midseason, 70–80 days after transplanting

HEAT LEVEL Mild

Squat bell-like pods from this variety are earthy and, when dried, make great brown powders mostly for use in mole sauces.

Chilhuacle Rojo

Capsicum annuum 'Chilhuacle Rojo'

ORIGIN Mexico (Oaxaca)

PODS 3–4 in. long, 1.5–2 in. wide; pendant, green to deep maroon red

PLANT HEIGHT 18–24 in.

HARVEST Midseason, 70–80 days after transplanting

HEAT LEVEL Mild

This is one of the rarer Oaxacan chiles and is used in the traditional red mole, one of the seven Oaxacan moles.

Mulato Isleno

Capsicum annuum **'Mulato Isleno'**

ORIGIN Mexico

PODS 4–6 in. long, 1.5–1.75 in. wide; pendant, deep green to dark brown

PLANT HEIGHT 24–30 in.

HARVEST Midseason, 70–80 days after transplanting

HEAT LEVEL Mild

Pods are most frequently roasted and peeled; they make excellent chiles rellenos.

Tiburón Hybrid

Capsicum annuum **'Tiburón Hybrid'**

ORIGIN United States

PODS 5–7 in. long, 2.5–3.5 in. wide; pendant, dark green to red

PLANT HEIGHT 24–30 in.

HARVEST Midseason, 70–80 days after transplanting

HEAT LEVEL Medium

A newer, hotter hybrid variety; resistant to bacterial spot and tobacco mosaic virus (TMV). Used for stuffing.

Asian

Many of the Asian chiles are similar to the popular 'Thai Red' variety, with multiple stems, a compact to erect habit, and a mature height of 18–24 inches. Plants have medium green leaves, and the flower corollas are white with no spots. Pods are borne upright, several clustered at each node, and elongate and pointed, measuring up to 2½–3 inches long and ¼ inch wide. The growing period is 90 days or more. Some Asian varieties produce pendant pods. Most of the Asian peppers are rated between 30,000 and 100,000 SHUs. Note that there is a greater pod-shape diversity in this pod type because the geographic region is so vast.

Chile peppers found their way into Asia through India, and the initial responsibility for that goes to the Portuguese. Under the leadership of Alfonzo de Albuquerque, the Portuguese conquered the city of Goa on the Malabar Coast in 1510 and gained control of the spice trade. Goa was rich in spices—cloves, cinnamon, cardamom, ginger, and black pepper—which were shipped to Lisbon in return for silver and copper. Shortly after the fall of Goa it is suspected that chile peppers were introduced there by way of trade routes with Lisbon. Because of their familiarity with all kinds of pungent spices, the Indians of the Malabar Coast were undoubtedly quite taken with the fiery pods, and planted seeds that had been imported from monks' gardens on the Iberian Peninsula.

By 1542, three varieties of chiles were recognized in India, according to Dutch botanist Charles Clusius, and by the middle of that century chiles were extensively cultivated and exported. The chiles introduced into India were capsicums from the West Indies, the first chiles grown in Spain and Portugal. This theory is supported by the fact that *Capsicum annuum* became the most extensively cultivated chile in India and its main capsicum of commerce. From India, chiles moved eastward.

Although hard evidence is lacking, ethnobotanists theorize that Indian, Arab, or Portuguese traders—or some combination of them—carried chiles from India to Malacca, on the Malay Peninsula across from Sumatra, between 1510 and the late 1520s. From there, Portuguese traders introduced the fiery fruits into Thailand,

and numerous trading groups took them to Java, Sumatra, New Guinea, Macao, and the Philippines.

From the varieties present today in the region, it appears that the *C. annuum* and *C. frutescens* species were the primary chiles transferred to the region. But whichever species, chiles quickly became an important element in the cuisines of all the countries in the region. As Thai-food expert Jennifer Brennan described the process, chile peppers were "adopted by the Thai with a fervor normally associated with the return of a long-lost child."

In 1529, a treaty between Spain and Portugal gave the Spanish control of the Philippines and the Portuguese control of Malaysia. Since the Spanish also controlled Mexico, it was easier to administer the Philippines from there, so regular shipping routes between Manila and Acapulco were established. Mexican chiles and other foodstuffs were transferred directly from the New World to the Old across the Pacific.

By 1550, chiles had become well established in Southeast Asia, probably spread as much by birds as by human trade and cultivation. It is an ironic culinary fact that the imported chiles became as important as many traditional spices in Southeast Asian cuisines, thus illustrating how the pungency of chiles has been combined with indigenous flavors to fire up most of the cuisines of the region.

Chiles are most predominant in Southeast Asia, particularly Thailand, as well as Korea, western China, and the Spice Islands of Indonesia and Malaysia. They play a lesser role in the agriculture and cuisines of two other important Asian countries, Japan and the Philippines.

Capsicums were introduced into Japan in the late 1500s or early 1600s and were used as a vegetable, spice, and ornamental plant. By the late 1800s, cultivation was extensive, and the Japanese varieties known as 'Santaka' and 'Hontaka' became famous for their high pungency. Today, a mere 350 acres are planted for chile peppers, less than $\frac{1}{30}$th of the total capsicum acreage (the Japanese are more fond of bell peppers). In the Philippines, "hot pepper is a minor crop," according to one agricultural expert. Production is limited to very small, scattered areas and the most popular variety is 'Matikis'. *Capsicum frutescens* 'Siling Labuyo' is an extremely hot "bird pepper" that grows both wild and cultivated.

Achar

Capsicum annuum 'Achar'

ORIGIN India

PODS 3–4 in. long, 0.75–1 in. wide; pendant, green to deep red

PLANT HEIGHT 18–24 in.

HARVEST Midseason, 70–80 days after transplanting

HEAT LEVEL Mild

Achar is a generic term for chile peppers in India, and also the name of a spicy pickle, so it's not surprising that some plant breeder used the same word to name a variety. In addition to pickles, this variety would be common in Indian curries.

Afghan

Capsicum annuum 'Afghan'

ORIGIN Afghanistan

PODS 2.5–3 in. long, 0.375–0.5 in. wide; upright, green to red

PLANT HEIGHT 30–36 in.

HARVEST Midseason, 70–80 days after transplanting

HEAT LEVEL Hot

Used in Afghan spice rubs, and korma and kebab sauces.

Burning Bush

Capsicum annuum 'Burning Bush'

ORIGIN Unknown

PODS 2–4 in. long, 0.25–0.375 in. wide; upright, green to red

PLANT HEIGHT 24–30 in.

HARVEST Midseason, 70–80 days after transplanting

HEAT LEVEL Hot

Used in various spicy Asian cuisines such as Sichuan and Thai. Not to be confused with *C. chinense* 'Burning Bush'.

Cabai Burong

Capsicum annuum **'Cabai Burong'**

ORIGIN Malaysia

PODS 2–2.5 in. long, 0.25–0.375 in. wide; upright, green to red

PLANT HEIGHT 36–42 in.

HARVEST Midseason, 70–80 days after transplanting

HEAT LEVEL Hot

The varietal name means "bird pepper" in Malay. This variety is used in Malaysian and Indonesian dishes like curries that are variously called gulais and rendangs.

Chi-Chien

Capsicum annuum **'Chi-Chien'**

ORIGIN Unknown

PODS 2.5–3 in. long, 0.25–0.375 in. wide; upright, green to dark red

PLANT HEIGHT 18–24 in.

HARVEST Midseason, 70–80 days after transplanting

HEAT LEVEL Very hot

Used in Sichuan and Hunan dishes.

Dhanraj

Capsicum annuum **'Dhanraj'**

ORIGIN India

PODS 2–2.5 in. long, 0.375–0.5 in. wide; upright, green to red

PLANT HEIGHT 24–30 in.

HARVEST Midseason, 70–80 days after transplanting

HEAT LEVEL Medium

Cluster type. Used in Indian cuisine.

Hanoi Red

Capsicum annuum **'Hanoi Red'**

ORIGIN Vietnam

PODS 1.25–1.75 in. long, 0.25–0.5 in. wide; upright, green to red

PLANT HEIGHT 24–30 in.

HARVEST Midseason, 70–80 days after transplanting

HEAT LEVEL Very hot

Used in stir-fries and other spicy Southeast Asian dishes.

Indian P-C1

Capsicum annuum 'Indian P-C1'

ORIGIN India

PODS 2-2.5 in. long, 0.25-0.375 in. wide; upright to pendant, green to red

PLANT HEIGHT 18-24 in.

HARVEST Very late season, 90 or more days after transplanting

HEAT LEVEL Very hot

Also known as 'Indian PC-1'. Very prolific. Used in curries, chutneys, and pickles.

Indonesian

Capsicum annuum 'Indonesian'

ORIGIN Indonesia

PODS 4-5 in. wide, 0.25-0.375 in. long; pendant, green to red

PLANT HEIGHT 24-30 in.

HARVEST Midseason, 70-80 days after transplanting

HEAT LEVEL Hot

Used in Malaysian and Indonesian dishes like curries that are variously called gulais and rendangs.

Kung Pao Hybrid

Capsicum annuum **'Kung Pao Hybrid'**

ORIGIN Probably United States

PODS 4–5 in. long, 0.375–0.5 in. wide; pendant, green to bright red

PLANT HEIGHT 24–30 in.

HARVEST Midseason, 70–80 days after transplanting

HEAT LEVEL Hot

Prolific. Used in stir-fries, pickles, and hot sauces.

Laotian

Capsicum annuum **'Laotian'**

ORIGIN Laos

PODS 1.5–2 in. long, 0.25–0.375 in. wide; upright to pendant, green to red

PLANT HEIGHT 18-24 in.

HARVEST Midseason, 70–80 days after transplanting

HEAT LEVEL Hot

Used in hot curries, stir-fries, and grilling sauces.

New Delhi Long

Capiscum annuum **'New Delhi Long'**

ORIGIN India

PODS 3–4 in. long, 0.375–0.5 in. wide; pendant, green to red

PLANT HEIGHT 18–24 in.

HARVEST Midseason, 70–80 days after transplanting

HEAT LEVEL Hot

Used in Indian foods such as curries, chutneys, and pickles.

Punjab Small Hot

Capiscum annuum **'Punjab Small Hot'**

ORIGIN India

PODS 2–3 in. long, 0.25–0.375 in. wide; pendant, green to red

PLANT HEIGHT 24–30 in.

HARVEST Midseason, 70–80 days after transplanting

HEAT LEVEL Very hot

Used in Indian foods such as curries, chutneys, and pickles.

Salmon

Capsicum annuum 'Salmon'

ORIGIN Unknown

PODS 1.5–2 in. long, 0.25–0.375 in. wide; upright, green to red

PLANT HEIGHT 18–24 in.

HARVEST Late season, 80–90 days after transplanting

HEAT LEVEL Hot

Used dried and in Asian cuisine.

Shishito

Capsicum annuum 'Shishito'

ORIGIN Japan

PODS 3–4 in. long, 0.5–0.75 in. wide; pendant, green to red

PLANT HEIGHT 12–18 in.

HARVEST Early season, 60–70 days after transplanting

HEAT LEVEL Sweet

Used in Japanese cuisine as a salad ingredient and garnish, as well as for tempura.

Suryankhi Cluster

Capsicum annuum 'Suryankhi Cluster'

ORIGIN India

PODS 1.5–2.5 in. long, 0.25–0.375 in. wide; upright, green to red

PLANT HEIGHT 18–24 in.

HARVEST Midseason, 70–80 days after transplanting

HEAT LEVEL Very hot

Used in Indian foods such as curries, chutneys, and pickles.

Szechwan

Capsicum annuum 'Szechwan'

ORIGIN China

PODS 3.5–4.5 in. long, 0.25–0.375 in. wide; pendant, green to red

PLANT HEIGHT 24–30 in.

HARVEST Midseason, 70–80 days after transplanting

HEAT LEVEL Hot

Used in stir-fries, pickles, and other Chinese dishes.

Takanotsume

Capsicum annuum 'Takanotsume'

ORIGIN Japan

PODS 2–3 in. long, 0.25–0.375 in. wide; upright, green to red

PLANT HEIGHT 18-24 in.

HARVEST Midseason, 70–80 days after transplanting

HEAT LEVEL Very hot

One of the most popular chiles in Japan; used in many Asian cuisines.

Tejaswini Hybrid

Capsicum annuum **'Tejaswini Hybrid'**

ORIGIN India

PODS 3–3.5 in. long, 0.375–0.5 in. wide; pendant, green to red

PLANT HEIGHT 24–30 in.

HARVEST Midseason, 70–80 days after transplanting

HEAT LEVEL Hot

Prolific. Used in Indian foods such as curries, chutneys, and pickles.

Thai Giant

Capsicum annuum 'Thai Giant'

ORIGIN Thailand

PODS 1.5–2 in. long, 0.5–0.75 in. wide; upright becoming pendant, green to red

PLANT HEIGHT 12–18 in.

HARVEST Midseason, 70–80 days after transplanting

HEAT LEVEL Very hot

Twice the flesh of other Thai varieties; used in Asian cuisines and curries.

Thai Red

Capsicum annuum 'Thai Red'

ORIGIN Thailand

PODS 2.25–2.5 in. long, 0.25–0.375 in. wide; upright, green to red

PLANT HEIGHT 18–24 in.

HARVEST Very late, 90 or more days after transplanting

HEAT LEVEL Very hot

Used in Southeast Asian foods such as curries and stir-fries.

Thai Yellow

Capsicum annuum 'Thai Yellow'

ORIGIN Thailand

PODS 2.25–2.5 in. long, 0.25–0.375 in. wide; upright, green to golden yellow

PLANT HEIGHT 18–24 in.

HARVEST Very late season, 90 or more days after transplanting

HEAT LEVEL Very hot

Used in Southeast Asian foods such as curries and stir-fries.

Yatsufusa

Capsicum annuum 'Yatsufusa'

ORIGIN Japan

PODS 2–3 in. long, 0.25–0.375 in. wide; upright, green to red

PLANT HEIGHT 18–24 in.

HARVEST Midseason, 70–80 days after transplanting

HEAT LEVEL Hot

'Yatsufusa' is a hot specialty pepper that is also known as 'Chiles Japones'. The mature, dried fruits are ground and used in *shichimi togarashi* (Japanese seven spice), a popular condiment.

Bell

Bells are the most commonly grown commercial peppers in the United States, with approximately 65,000 acres under cultivation. Mexico follows with about 22,000 acres, and most of their bells are exported to the United States. More than 100 varieties of bell peppers have been bred, and we have chosen our selections here on the basis of their popularity and availability to the home grower.

Bell peppers are multistemmed with a habit that is subcompact tending toward prostrate, growing between 1 and 2½ feet tall. The leaves are medium green, ovate to lanceolate, and smooth. The flower corollas are white with no spots. The pods are pendant, 3-or 4-lobed, blocky, and blunt, ranging from 3–7 inches long and 2–4 inches wide. Their immature color is usually dark green, maturing to red, but sometimes to yellow, orange, or purple. The pungent variety, 'Mexi-Bell', has only a slight bite, ranging from 100 to 400 SHUs.

Bells grow well in sandy loams with good drainage. The growing period ranges from 80 to 100 days after transplanting, depending on whether the plants are directly seeded or transplanted and whether the pods are picked green or at the mature color. If fertilized correctly, bells are heavy feeders. Most bells are used in the fresh form, cut up in salads or stuffed and baked. Pungent bells are also used in fresh salsas. Both kinds can be preserved by freezing.

———————————————

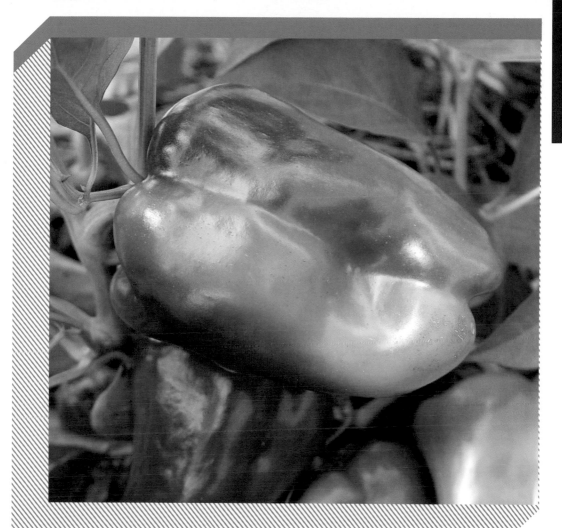

Ace Hybrid

Capsicum annuum **'Ace Hybrid'**

ORIGIN United States

PODS 4–5 in. long, 3–4 in. wide; pendant, green to red

PLANT HEIGHT 18–24 in.

HARVEST Early season, 60–70 days after transplanting

HEAT LEVEL Sweet

A good early bell for cool-season climates.

Albino

Capsicum annuum 'Albino'

ORIGIN United States

PODS 4–4.5 in. long, 2–2.5 in. wide; upright to pendant, pale yellow to orange to red

PLANT HEIGHT 12–18 in.

HARVEST Early season, 60–70 days after transplanting

HEAT LEVEL Sweet

Pods have more of a blocky shape. Used in Italian cuisine and for stuffing, roasting, frying, and in stir-fries.

Bell Boy Hybrid

Capsicum annuum 'Bell Boy Hybrid'

ORIGIN United States

PODS 3.5–4.5 in. long, 3–4 in. wide; pendant, green to red

PLANT HEIGHT 18–24 in.

HARVEST Early season, 60–70 days after transplanting

HEAT LEVEL Sweet

A dependable bell; resistant to tobacco mosaic virus. A good variety for stuffing.

Big Bertha Hybrid

Capsicum annuum 'Big Bertha Hybrid'

ORIGIN United States

PODS 6-7 in. long, 3-4 in. wide; pendant, green to bright red

PLANT HEIGHT 24-30 in.

HARVEST Midseason, 70-80 days after transplanting

HEAT LEVEL Sweet

Resistant to tobacco mosaic virus. Huge pods are used for stuffing.

Big Red

Capsicum annuum 'Big Red'

ORIGIN United States

PODS 3-5 in. long, 3-4 in. wide; pendant, green to red

PLANT HEIGHT 18-24 in.

HARVEST Midseason, 70-80 days after transplanting

HEAT LEVEL Sweet

Heirloom variety. Excellent in salads.

Blushing Beauty Hybrid

Capsicum annuum **'Blushing Beauty Hybrid'**

ORIGIN United States

PODS 3.5–4 in. long and wide; pendant, pale yellow to apricot-orange to red

PLANT HEIGHT 18–24 in.

HARVEST Early season, 60–70 days after transplanting

HEAT LEVEL Sweet

All America Selections winner. This bell is never green. Resistant to three viruses and bacterial leaf spot. Sweet, crispy flesh.

Bull Nose

Capsicum annuum **'Bull Nose'**

ORIGIN India, United States

PODS 3.5–4.5 in. long, 3–3.5 in. wide; pendant, green to red

PLANT HEIGHT 18–24 in. tall

HARVEST Midseason, 70–80 days after transplanting

HEAT LEVEL Sweet

The original bull nose pepper was popular in colonial America and was grown by Thomas Jefferson—in fact, they are still grown at Monticello today. Uniform fruits; sometimes the inner ribs have a tinge of heat.

California Wonder

Capsicum annuum 'California Wonder'

ORIGIN United States

PODS 4–5 in. long, 3–4 in. wide; pendant, green to red

PLANT HEIGHT 18-24 in.

HARVEST Midseason, 70–80 days after transplanting

HEAT LEVEL Sweet

Resistant to tobacco mosaic virus. This is probably the most popular of all the open-pollinated bells for both commercial growers and home gardeners.

Calwonder Golden

Capsicum annuum 'Calwonder Golden'

ORIGIN United States

PODS 4–5 in. long, 3–4 in. wide; pendant, green to golden yellow

PLANT HEIGHT 18-24 in.

HARVEST Midseason, 70–80 days after transplanting

HEAT LEVEL Sweet

Golden yellow color is stunning in salads, and the whole pods may be stuffed.

Chinese Giant

Capsicum annuum 'Chinese Giant'

ORIGIN United States

PODS 4–6 in. long, 3–4 in. wide; pendant, green to bright red

PLANT HEIGHT 18–24 in.

HARVEST Midseason, 70–80 days after transplanting

HEAT LEVEL Sweet

Not Chinese but an American heirloom. Used for stuffing; great flavor.

Chocolate Beauty Hybrid

Capsicum annuum 'Chocolate Beauty Hybrid'

ORIGIN United States

PODS 3.5–4 in. long, 3–4 in. wide; pendant, green to mahogany brown

PLANT HEIGHT 18–24 in.

HARVEST Early season, 60–70 days after transplanting

HEAT LEVEL Sweet

Prolific; resistant to tobacco mosaic virus. A nice brown "chocolate" bell.

Corona

Capsicum annuum 'Corona'

ORIGIN Unknown

PODS 3–4 in. long and wide; pendant, green to orange

PLANT HEIGHT 18–24 in.

HARVEST Midseason, 70–80 days after transplanting

HEAT LEVEL Sweet

Resistant to tobacco mosaic virus. Very sweet and good in salads.

Diamond

Capsicum annuum 'Diamond'

ORIGIN United States

PODS 3–4 in. long, 3–3.5 in. wide; upright to pendant, translucent white to yellow to orange to scarlet red

PLANT HEIGHT 12–18 in.

HARVEST Early season, 60–70 days after transplanting

HEAT LEVEL Sweet

Harvest while translucent white and julienne in combination with green, red, orange, and yellow peppers with thinly sliced red onions for a rainbow-colored salad dressed with any kind of vinaigrette.

Early Sunsation Hybrid

Capsicum annuum **'Early Sunsation Hybrid'**

ORIGIN United States

PODS 3.5–4.5 in. long, 3–4 in. wide; pendant, green to bright yellow

PLANT HEIGHT 24–30 in.

HARVEST Midseason, 70–80 days after transplanting

HEAT LEVEL Sweet

Resistant to bacterial leaf spot. One of the largest yellow bells you can grow.

Karma Hybrid

Capsicum annuum **'Karma Hybrid'**

ORIGIN United States

PODS 5–6 in. long, 3–4 in. wide; pendant, green to red

PLANT HEIGHT 18–24 in.

HARVEST Midseason, 70–80 days after transplanting

HEAT LEVEL Sweet

Prolific; plants may need staking. Extremely flavorful.

King Arthur Hybrid

Capsicum annuum **'King Arthur Hybrid'**

ORIGIN United States

PODS 3.5–4.5 in. long, 3.5–4 in. wide; pendant, green to red

PLANT HEIGHT 18–24 in.

HARVEST Midseason, 70–80 days after transplanting

HEAT LEVEL Sweet

Disease resistant. Good combination of early maturity and large fruit size. Previously named 'Fat 'N Sassy'.

King of the North

Capsicum annuum 'King of the North'

ORIGIN United States

PODS 4–5 in. long, 3.5–4 in. wide; pendant, green to red

PLANT HEIGHT 18–24 in.

HARVEST Early season, 60–70 days after transplanting

HEAT LEVEL Sweet

Dependable cool-season garden variety; uniform fruits. Good for stuffing.

Lady Bell Hybrid

Capsicum annuum 'Lady Bell Hybrid'

ORIGIN United States

PODS 3–4 in. long and wide; pendant, green to red

PLANT HEIGHT 18–24 in.

HARVEST Early season, 60–70 days after transplanting

HEAT LEVEL Sweet

Prolific; a good producer of slightly smaller bells. Stuffed and used in salads.

Lamuyo

Capsicum annuum 'Lamuyo'

ORIGIN United States

PODS 5–6 in. long, 2.5–3 in. wide; pendant, green to red

PLANT HEIGHT 24–30 in.

HARVEST Midseason, 70–80 days after transplanting

HEAT LEVEL Sweet

Also known as 'Lido Lamuyo'.

La Rouge Royale

Capsicum annuum 'La Rouge Royale'

ORIGIN United States

PODS 5–7 in. long, 3–3.5 in. wide; pendant, green to red

PLANT HEIGHT 24–30 in.

HARVEST Midseason, 70–80 days after transplanting

HEAT LEVEL Sweet

Huge pods can be stuffed and then sliced for serving.

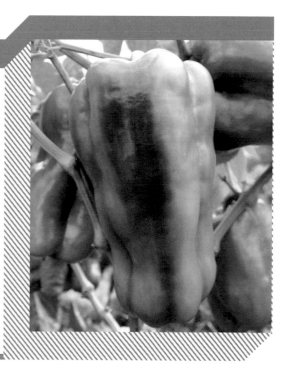

Mavras Hybrid

Capsicum annuum **'Mavras Hybrid'**

ORIGIN United States

PODS 3-5 in. long, 3-4 in. wide; pendant, black to purple to red

PLANT HEIGHT 18-24 in.

HARVEST Midseason, 70-80 days after transplanting

HEAT LEVEL Sweet

Resistant to tobacco mosaic virus. A black bell!

Mexi-Belle Hybrid

Capsicum annuum **'Mexi-Belle Hybrid'**

ORIGIN United States

PODS 3-4 in. long, 2.5-3.5 in. wide; pendant, green to red

PLANT HEIGHT 18-24 in.

HARVEST Early season, 60-70 days after transplanting

HEAT LEVEL Mild

Resistant to tobacco mosaic virus. A bell with a touch of heat; used for stuffing.

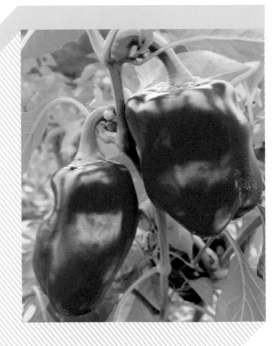

Mini Chocolate Bell

Capsicum annuum **'Mini Chocolate Bell'**

ORIGIN United States

PODS 1.25–1.75 in. long, 1–1.5 in. wide; upright, green to chocolate brown

PLANT HEIGHT 12–18 in.

HARVEST Midseason, 70–80 days after transplanting

HEAT LEVEL Sweet

Tiny bells used for snacking or stuffing.

Mini Red Bell

Capsicum annuum **'Mini Red Bell'**

ORIGIN United States

PODS 1–1.5 in. long and wide; upright to pendant, green to red

PLANT HEIGHT 12–18 in.

HARVEST Early season, 60–70 days after transplanting

HEAT LEVEL Sweet

Stuff these tiny bells with a variety of cheeses for a unique appetizer.

Mini Yellow Bell

Capsicum annuum **'Mini Yellow Bell'**

ORIGIN United States

PODS 1–1.5 in. long and wide; upright to pendant, green to yellow

PLANT HEIGHT 12–18 in.

HARVEST Early season, 60–70 days after transplanting

HEAT LEVEL Sweet

Makes a good snacking pepper, and can be stuffed for an appetizer.

Orange Sun

Capsicum annuum 'Orange Sun'

ORIGIN United States

PODS 3.5–4.5 in. long, 3–4 in. wide; pendant, green to orange

PLANT HEIGHT 18–24 in.

HARVEST Early season, 60–70 days after transplanting

HEAT LEVEL Sweet

A lovely orange bell ideal for grilling, sautéing, and stuffing. Also good when fresh.

Patriot Hybrid

Capsicum annuum 'Patriot Hybrid'

ORIGIN United States

PODS 4–5 in. long, 3.5–4.5 in. wide; pendant, green to red

PLANT HEIGHT 24–30 in.

HARVEST Midseason, 70–80 days after transplanting

HEAT LEVEL Sweet

Disease resistant; a dependable producer.

Purple Beauty

Capsicum annuum 'Purple Beauty'

ORIGIN United States

PODS 3–4 in. long, 2.5–3 in. wide; pendant, green to dark purple to red

PLANT HEIGHT 18–24 in.

HARVEST Early season, 60–70 days after transplanting

HEAT LEVEL Sweet

As purple as an eggplant! Makes an eye-catching addition to salads.

Quadrato D'asti Giallo

Capsicum annuum 'Quadrato D'asti Giallo'

ORIGIN Italy

PODS 6–7 in. long, 3.5–4 in. wide; pendant, green to golden yellow

PLANT HEIGHT 24–30 in.

HARVEST Midseason, 70–80 days after transplanting

HEAT LEVEL Sweet

A frying pepper used in Italian cuisine, or used fresh.

Quadrato D'asti Rosso

Capsicum annuum 'Quadrato D'asti Rosso'

ORIGIN Italy

PODS 6–7 in. long, 3.5–4 in. wide; pendant, green to red

PLANT HEIGHT 24–30 in.

HARVEST Midseason, 70–80 days after transplanting

HEAT LEVEL Sweet

A frying pepper used in Italian cuisine, or used fresh.

Red Beauty Hybrid

Capsicum annuum 'Red Beauty Hybrid'

ORIGIN United States

PODS 4–5 in. long, 3–4 in. wide; pendant, green to red

PLANT HEIGHT 18–24 in.

HARVEST Midseason, 70–80 days after transplanting

HEAT LEVEL Sweet

Heavy yields; resistant to tobacco mosaic virus. Very thick walled; can be stuffed.

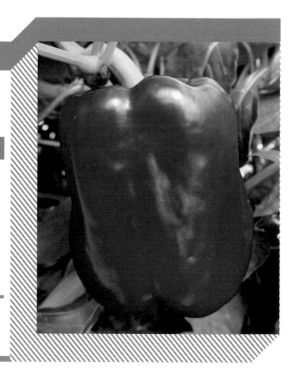

Sunbright

Capsicum annuum 'Sunbright'

ORIGIN United States

PODS 3–4 in. long and wide; pendant, green to bright yellow

PLANT HEIGHT 18-24 in.

HARVEST Early season, 60–70 days after transplanting

HEAT LEVEL Sweet

A good dependable yellow bell.

Sunrise Orange Sweet

Capsicum annuum 'Sunrise Orange Sweet'

ORIGIN United States

PODS 3.5–4.5 in. long, 2.5–3.5 in. wide; pendant, pale yellow to orange-blushed to red

PLANT HEIGHT 18–24 in.

HARVEST Early season, 60–70 days after transplanting

HEAT LEVEL Sweet

Resistant to tobacco mosaic virus. Very sweet and juicy; beautiful as it goes through color changes.

Super Heavyweight Hybrid

Capsicum annuum 'Super Heavyweight Hybrid'

ORIGIN United States

PODS 4–5 in. long and wide; pendant, green to golden yellow

PLANT HEIGHT 24–30 in.

HARVEST Midseason, 70–80 days after transplanting

HEAT LEVEL Sweet

One of the largest bell peppers in the world; plants will need to be staked to ensure branches don't break with the heavy fruits.

Cayenne

The word *cayenne* seems to come from *kian*, the name of the pepper among the Tupi Indians of northeastern South America. The pod type probably originated in what is now French Guiana and was named after either the Cayenne River or the capital of the country, Cayenne.

It owes its spread around the world to Portugal, whose traders carried it to Europe, Africa, India, and Asia. Although it probably was introduced into Spain before 1500, its circuitous route caused it to be introduced into Britain from India in 1548.

A plant resembling cayenne was described in 1552 in the Aztec herbal *The Badanius Manuscript,* indicating their medical use for such hot peppers: treating toothaches and scabies. In 1597, the botanist John Gerard referred to cayenne as "ginnie or Indian pepper" in his herbal, and in his influential herbal of 1652, Nicholas Culpepper wrote that cayenne was "this violent fruit" that was of considerable service to "help digestion, provoke urine, relieve toothache, preserve the teeth from rottenness, comfort a cold stomach, expel the stone from the kidney, and take away dimness of sight." Cayenne appeared in *Miller's Garden Dictionary* in 1771, proving it was cultivated in England—at least in home gardens.

The cayenne plant is treelike, with multiple stems and an erect habit. It grows up to 3 feet tall and 2 feet wide. The leaves are ovate, smooth, and medium green. The flower corollas are white with no spots. The pods are pendant, long, and slender, measuring up to 10 inches long and 1 inch wide. They are often wrinkled and irregular in shape. The cayenne is very pungent, measuring between 30,000 and 50,000 SHUs.

Grown commercially in New Mexico, Louisiana, Africa, India, Japan, and Mexico, the cayenne has a growing period of about 90 days after transplanting. Surprisingly, perhaps, New Mexico is leading the way in production of cayenne chiles for hot sauces, according to Gene Jefferies, formerly of the McIlhenny Company, which owns Trappey's, a major cayenne sauce manufacturer. In

1995, more than 1000 acres of cayenne were planted in New Mexico. Cayenne acreage in the United States rose from 2500 acres in 1994 to 4500 acres in 1995. About 105 million pounds of cayenne mash (crushed cayennes with about 20 percent salt) was produced in the United States, with Reckitt Benckiser, producers of Frank's Red Hot, accounting for nearly half of that amount. In fact, 75–85 percent of all cayenne mash in the world is produced in the United States. Retail sales (not including food service) of cayenne pepper sauces topped $82 million in 1995.

Although cayennes can be used fresh in the immature green form in salsas, the most common use is to grind the dried red pods into a powder. In Louisiana, numerous hot sauces are made with cayennes.

Keep in mind that although the name *cayenne* is commonly used in commerce, the cayenne you buy may not be made from the cayenne pod type—in fact, it probably is not. Virtually any small, hot red chile can be ground and placed in a capsule and called cayenne. That said, this is not necessarily a bad thing, as there's no difference in the composition of the different pod types and varieties of the *C. annuum* species, except in heat level. In summary, a capsule of ground piquín pods will virtually be the same in chemical composition as a capsule of ground cayenne pods. In fact, the American Spice Trade Association considers the term *cayenne* to be a misnomer and prefers the more generic term *red pepper.*

Berbere

Capsicum annuum 'Berbere'

ORIGIN Ethiopia

PODS 3-4 in. long, 0.5-0.75 in. wide; upright to pendant, green to orange to red

PLANT HEIGHT 24-30 in.

HARVEST Midseason, 70-80 days after transplanting

HEAT LEVEL Medium

Here is a chile nomenclature anomaly: a pepper variety named after the spice mixture it appears in. That's because *berbere* is the Amharic word for chile pepper and the spice mixture used to season meat.

Cayenne Buist's Yellow

Capsicum annuum 'Cayenne Buist's Yellow'

ORIGIN United States

PODS 4-5 in. long, 0.75-1 in. wide; pendant, green to dark golden orange

PLANT HEIGHT 18-24 in.

HARVEST Midseason, 70-80 days after transplanting

HEAT LEVEL Hot

Used dried, for chile powder, and in fresh salsas.

Cayenne Carolina

Capsicum annuum **'Cayenne Carolina'**

ORIGIN United States, South Carolina

PODS 5–6 in. long, 0.75–1 in. wide; pendant, green to red

PLANT HEIGHT 24–30 in.

HARVEST Midseason, 70–80 days after transplanting

HEAT LEVEL Hot

Also known as 'Carolina Cayenne'. Used dried, for chile powder, and in fresh salsas; twice the heat of a normal cayenne.

Cayenne Golden

Capsicum annuum **'Cayenne Golden'**

ORIGIN United States

PODS 5–6 in. long, 0.75–1 in. wide; pendant, green to golden yellow

PLANT HEIGHT 18–24 in.

HARVEST Midseason, 70–80 days after transplanting

HEAT LEVEL Hot

Also known as 'Golden Cayenne'. Used dried, to make a golden yellow powder, and in fresh salsas.

Cayenne Large Thick

Capsicum annuum **'Cayenne Large Thick'**

ORIGIN United States

PODS 5–6 in. long, 0.75–1 in. wide; pendant, green to red

PLANT HEIGHT 18–24 in.

HARVEST Midseason, 70–80 days after transplanting

HEAT LEVEL Hot

Also known as 'Large Thick Cayenne'. Used dried, for chile powder, in fresh salsas, and for pickling.

Cayenne Long Slim

Capsicum annuum **'Cayenne Long Slim'**

ORIGIN United States

PODS 4–6 in. long, 0.375–0.5 in. wide; pendant, green to red

PLANT HEIGHT 18–24 in.

HARVEST Midseason, 70–80 days after transplanting

HEAT LEVEL Hot

Also known as 'Long Slim Cayenne'. Fruits are often curled and twisted. Used dried, for chile powders, in fresh salsas, and for pickling.

Cayenne Purple

Capsicum annuum 'Cayenne Purple'

ORIGIN United States

PODS 3.5–4.5 in. long, 0.375–0.5 in. wide; pendant, green to purple to red

PLANT HEIGHT 18–24 in.

HARVEST Midseason, 70–80 days after transplanting

HEAT LEVEL Hot

Also known as 'Purple Cayenne'. Used dried, for chile powder, and in fresh salsas.

Cayenne Sweet

Capsicum annuum **'Cayenne Sweet'**

ORIGIN United States

PODS 7–9 in. long, 0.5–0.75 in. wide; pendant, green to orange to red

PLANT HEIGHT 18–24 in.

HARVEST Midseason, 70–80 days after transplanting

HEAT LEVEL Sweet

Also known as 'Sweet Cayenne'. Prolific; pods curve into a near circle. Used dried, for chile powder, and in fresh salsas.

Charleston Hot

Capsicum annuum 'Charleston Hot'

ORIGIN United States (South Carolina)

PODS 4–5 in. long, 0.75–1 in. wide; pendant, pale green to yellow to orange to red

PLANT HEIGHT 18–24 in.

HARVEST Midseason, 70–80 days after transplanting

HEAT LEVEL Very hot

Prolific; plants have yellowish foliage. Used dried, for chile powder, in fresh salsas, and for pickling.

Cobra

Capsicum annuum 'Cobra'

ORIGIN India

PODS 5–6 in. long, 0.375–0.5 in. wide; pendant, green to red

PLANT HEIGHT 18–24 in.

HARVEST Midseason, 70–80 days after transplanting

HEAT LEVEL Very hot

Prolific. Used dried, for chile powder, and in Indian cuisine.

Corbaci

Capsicum annuum 'Corbaci'

ORIGIN Turkey

PODS 5-6 in. long, 0.5-0.75 in. wide; pendant, green to orange to red

PLANT HEIGHT 18-24 in.

HARVEST Early season, 60-70 days after transplanting

HEAT LEVEL Sweet

Prolific; pods twist and curl. Can be eaten fresh or used for chile powder.

Demre

Capsicum annuum 'Demre'

ORIGIN Turkey

PODS 4-6 in. long, 0.5-0.75 in. wide; pendant, green to orange to red

PLANT HEIGHT 18-24 in.

HARVEST Midseason, 70-80 days after transplanting

HEAT LEVEL Mild

A milder cayenne. Used dried, for chile powder, for pickling, in stir-fries, as fried peppers, or for a milder salsa.

Dragon's Claw

Capsicum annuum **'Dragon's Claw'**

ORIGIN India

PODS 8–10 in. long, 0.5–0.75 in. wide; pendant, green to deep red

PLANT HEIGHT 18–24 in.

HARVEST Midseason, 70–80 days after transplanting

HEAT LEVEL Medium

Used dried in crafting to make ristras, or as a powder.

Elephant Trunk

Capsicum annuum **'Elephant Trunk'**

ORIGIN India

PODS 5–7 in. long, 0.75–1 in. wide; pendant, pale green to red

PLANT HEIGHT 24–30 in.

HARVEST Midseason, 70–80 days after transplanting

HEAT LEVEL Medium

Used dried, for chile powder or crafting, and in Indian cuisine.

Garden Salsa Hybrid

Capsicum annuum **'Garden Salsa Hybrid'**

ORIGIN United States

PODS 8–9 in. long, 0.75–1 in. wide; pendant, green to red

PLANT HEIGHT 18–24 in.

HARVEST Midseason, 70–80 days after transplanting

HEAT LEVEL Medium

Prolific; resistant to tobacco mosaic virus. Used in fresh salsas.

Goat Horn

Capsicum annuum **'Goat Horn'**

ORIGIN Basque Country of Spain

PODS 4–5 in. long, 1–1.5 in. wide; pendant, green to red

PLANT HEIGHT 18–24 in.

HARVEST Midseason, 70–80 days after transplanting

HEAT LEVEL Medium

Also known as 'Sweet Spanish Long'. Used mostly in sauces, but also dried and for chile powder.

Hot Portugal

Capsicum annuum 'Hot Portugal'

ORIGIN Portugal

PODS 5–7 in. long, 0.75–1 in. wide; pendant, green to red

PLANT HEIGHT 18–24 in.

HARVEST Early season, 60–70 days after transplanting

HEAT LEVEL Hot

Used in roasting, canning, processing, and fried and stir-fried.

Iberia Hybrid

Capsicum annuum 'Iberia Hybrid'

ORIGIN United States

PODS 7–10 in. long, 1–1.5 in. wide; pendant, green to red

PLANT HEIGHT 24–30 in.

HARVEST Early season, 60–70 days after transplanting

HEAT LEVEL Medium

Used dried, in roasting, stir-fries, fried, and for crafts. A New Jersey Long Hot / Mesilla type.

Island Hellfire

Capsicum annuum **'Island Hellfire'**

ORIGIN Unknown

PODS 2–2.75 in. long, 0.25–0.5 in. wide; pendant, green to red

PLANT HEIGHT 30–36 in.

HARVEST Midseason, 70–80 days after transplanting

HEAT LEVEL Very hot

Used dried, for chile powder, and in fresh salsas.

Lombak

Capsicum annuum **'Lombak'**

ORIGIN Indonesia

PODS 5–6 in. long, 0.75–1 in. wide; pendant, green to red

PLANT HEIGHT 18–24 in.

HARVEST Midseason, 70–80 days after transplanting

HEAT LEVEL Mild

Heirloom. Used dried, for chile powder, and in Indonesian or Malaysian cuisine, especially in sauces.

Merah

Capsicum annuum 'Merah'

ORIGIN Malaysia

PODS 4–5 in. long, 0.75–1 in. wide; pendant, green to red

PLANT HEIGHT 18–24 in.

HARVEST Midseason, 70–80 days after transplanting

HEAT LEVEL Hot

Used dried, for chile powder, and in Indonesian or Malaysian cuisine, especially in sauces.

Mombasa

Capsicum annuum 'Mombasa'

ORIGIN Africa

PODS 4–6 in. long, 0.375–0.5 in. wide; pendant, green to red

PLANT HEIGHT 30–36 in.

HARVEST Midseason, 70–80 days after transplanting

HEAT LEVEL Hot

Used dried, for chile powder, and in fresh salsas.

Monkey Face

Capsicum annuum 'Monkey Face'

ORIGIN United States

PODS 4–5 in. long, 1–1.5 in. wide; pendant, green to red, sometimes green to golden yellow

PLANT HEIGHT 18–24 in.

HARVEST Midseason, 70–80 days after transplanting

HEAT LEVEL Hot

Unusually shaped fruit. Used for pickling.

Peter Orange

Capsicum annuum 'Peter Orange'

ORIGIN United States

PODS 3–4 in. long, 1–1.25 in. wide; pendant, green to chocolate brown

PLANT HEIGHT 18–24 in.

HARVEST Midseason, 70–80 days after transplanting

HEAT LEVEL Medium

A new color on an old variety. Used fresh in salsas.

Peter Red

Capsicum annuum 'Peter Red'

ORIGIN United States

PODS 3–4 in. long, 1–1.25 in. wide; pendant, green to red

PLANT HEIGHT 18–24 in.

HARVEST Midseason, 70–80 days after transplanting

HEAT LEVEL Hot

Good container plant. Its unusually shaped fruit (it is also known as "Penis Pepper") makes for great conversation. Used in fresh salsas.

Peter Yellow

Capsicum annuum 'Peter Yellow'

ORIGIN United States

PODS 3–4 in. long, 1–1.25 in. wide; pendant, green to yellow

PLANT HEIGHT 18–24 in.

HARVEST Midseason, 70–80 days after transplanting

HEAT LEVEL Medium

Good container plant with unusually shaped fruit. Used in fresh salsas.

Pico de Gallo

Capsicum annuum 'Pico de Gallo'

ORIGIN Mexico

PODS 1.5–1.75 in. long, 0.25–0.375 in. wide; pendant, green to brownish to red

PLANT HEIGHT 24–30 in.

HARVEST Midseason, 70–80 days after transplant

HEAT LEVEL Hot

Used fresh in salsas and dried in sauces and for chile powder.

Prik Chi Faa

Capsicum annuum 'Prik Chi Faa'

ORIGIN Thailand

PODS 3–5 in. long, 0.5–0.75 in. wide; pendant, green to red

PLANT HEIGHT 24–30 in.

HARVEST Midseason, 70–80 days after transplanting.

HEAT LEVEL Medium

Sometimes spelled 'Prik Chee Fa'. Used for chile powder and in Thai and other Asian dishes.

Ring of Fire

Capsicum annuum 'Ring of Fire'

ORIGIN United States

PODS 3–4 in. long, 0.25–0.375 in. wide; pendant, green to red

PLANT HEIGHT 18–24 in.

HARVEST Early season, 60–70 days after transplanting

HEAT LEVEL Hot

Used dried in sauces, for chile powder, and in fresh salsas.

Sugarchile Hybrid

Capsicum annuum 'Sugarchile Hybrid'

ORIGIN United States

PODS 5–6 in. long, 1–1.5 in. wide; pendant, green to red

PLANT HEIGHT 24–30 in.

HARVEST Midseason, 70–80 days after transplanting

HEAT LEVEL Mild

Prolific. Used as powder and for roasting and stuffing, frying, in stir-fries, as well as for canning and processing.

Cherry

This pod type was mentioned in botanical literature as early as 1586 and was illustrated in Besler's *Celeberrimi eystetensis*, an herbal published in 1613. It was introduced into England from the West Indies in 1759, and later transferred to the United States.

The plant has single to intermediate stems, an upright habit, and grows 12–24 inches tall. The leaves are dark green and smooth. The flower corollas are white with no spots. The pods are globelike, sometimes with a blunt point, and are borne either upright or pendant, or upright falling with their weight as they mature to become pendant. They measure 1½ inches long and 1¾ inches wide, and are brown or red at maturity. The heat level of this type varies considerably, from zero to about 3500 SHUs.

Cherry Bomb Hybrid

Capsicum annuum 'Cherry Bomb Hybrid'

ORIGIN United States

PODS 1.5–2 in. long and wide; pendant, green to red

PLANT HEIGHT 18–24 in.

HARVEST Midseason, 70–80 days after transplanting

HEAT LEVEL Medium

Prolific. Used in pickling, canning, processing, and for stuffing.

Cherry Chocolate

Capsicum annuum **'Cherry Chocolate'**

ORIGIN United States

PODS 1.5–2 in. long and wide; upright to pendant, green to dark brown

PLANT HEIGHT 18–24 in.

HARVEST Midseason, 70–80 days after transplanting

HEAT LEVEL Medium

A brown cherry. Used for stuffing.

Cherry Large Red

Capsicum annuum **'Cherry Large Red'**

ORIGIN United States

PODS 1.5–2 in. long and wide; upright to pendant, green to red

PLANT HEIGHT 18–24 in.

HARVEST Midseason, 70–80 days after transplanting

HEAT LEVEL Medium

Used in pickling, canning, processing, and for stuffing.

Cherry Sweet

Capsicum annuum 'Cherry Sweet'

ORIGIN United States

PODS 1.5–2 in. long and wide; pendant, green to red

PLANT HEIGHT 18–24 in.

HARVEST Midseason, 70–80 days after transplanting

HEAT LEVEL Sweet

A sweet cherry. Used in pickling, canning, processing, and for stuffing.

Cherry Tart

Capsicum annuum 'Cherry Tart'

ORIGIN United States

PODS 1–1.25 in. long and wide; pendant, green to red

PLANT HEIGHT 18–24 in.

HARVEST Midseason, 70–80 days after transplanting

HEAT LEVEL Medium

A smaller cherry. Used in pickling, canning, processing, and for stuffing.

Piccante Calabrese

Capsicum annuum **'Piccante Calabrese'**

ORIGIN Italy

PODS 1.25–1.75 in. long and wide; pendant, green to red

PLANT HEIGHT 24–30 in.

HARVEST Midseason, 70–80 days after transplanting

HEAT LEVEL Medium

Prolific. Used in pickling, canning, processing, and for stuffing.

Cuban

These sweet and mildly hot pods originated in Cuba and are much loved when fried. They include cubanelles and nardellos. Most Cuban varieties are nonpungent, although some may measure up to 500-1000 SHUs. The thin flesh of this type is very flavorful, so it has become a substitute for bells. The pods are used in salads, are pickled, and are usually fried or stuffed with meat and fried in Florida. Another common use for the Cuban varieties is sofrito (a sauce often used as a basis for beans, rice, and stews).

Plants have multiple stems and an erect habit, and grow to 24–30 inches. Leaves are ovate, smooth, and light to medium green. Flower corollas are white with no spots. The pods are pendant, long, and slender, measuring up to 2½ inches wide and 10 inches long. The immature pods are yellowish green, maturing to red.

Aconcagua

Capsicum annuum **'Aconcagua'**

ORIGIN Unknown

PODS 7–10 in. long, 2–2.5 in. wide; pendant, pale green to red

PLANT HEIGHT 24–30 in.

HARVEST Midseason, 70–80 days after transplanting

HEAT LEVEL Sweet

Named after the famous volcano. Plants have yellowish leaves. Used fresh and for stuffing and roasting, or fried and in stir-fries.

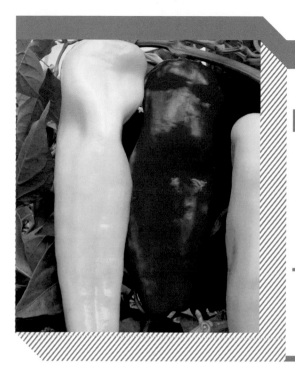

Biscayne Hybrid

Capsicum annuum 'Biscayne Hybrid'

ORIGIN United States

PODS 5–7 in. long, 1.5–2 in. wide; pendant, greenish yellow to red

PLANT HEIGHT 18–24 in.

HARVEST Midseason, 70–80 days after transplanting

HEAT LEVEL Sweet

Prolific. A cubanelle or Italian frying variant; best in stir-fries or eaten fresh.

Corno di Toro Red

Capsicum annuum 'Corno di Toro Red'

ORIGIN Italy

PODS 7–9 in. long, 1.5–2.5 in. wide; pendant, green to deep red

PLANT HEIGHT 24–30 in.

HARVEST Midseason, 70–80 days after transplanting

HEAT LEVEL Sweet

Shaped like a bull's horn. Used in Italian cuisine (especially sauces) and for roasting or frying and in stir-fries. Also used fresh in salads and salsas.

Corno Di Toro Yellow

Capsicum annuum 'Corno di Toro Yellow'

ORIGIN Italy

PODS 7–9 in. long, 1.5–2.5 in. wide; pendant, green to bright yellow

PLANT HEIGHT 24–30 in.

HARVEST Midseason, 70–80 days after transplanting

HEAT LEVEL Sweet

Shaped like a bull's horn. Used in Italian cuisine (especially sauces) and for salads, roasting, frying, and in stir-fries.

Cubanelle

Capsicum annuum 'Cubanelle'

ORIGIN Cuba and the United States

PODS 4–6 in. long, 1–1.5 in. wide; pendant, greenish yellow to deep red

PLANT HEIGHT 18–24 in. tall

HARVEST Midseason, 70–80 days after transplanting

HEAT LEVEL Sweet

Used in Italian and Latin American cuisines and for salads, roasting, frying, and in stir-fries. Also known as 'Sweet Italian Frying Pepper'.

Diablo Sweet

Capsicum annuum 'Diablo Sweet'

ORIGIN United States

PODS 8–9 in. long, 1.5–2 in. wide; pendant, green to red

PLANT HEIGHT 18–24 in.

HARVEST Midseason, 70–80 days after transplanting

HEAT LEVEL Sweet

Used in Italian and Latin American cuisines and for salads, roasting, frying, and in stir-fries.

Doux D'espagne

Capsicum annuum 'Doux D'espagne'

ORIGIN Spain

PODS 5–6 in. long, 2.5–3.5 in. wide; pendant, green to red

PLANT HEIGHT 24–30 in.

HARVEST Midseason, 70–80 days after transplanting

HEAT LEVEL Sweet

Large pods used in salads and for stuffing, roasting, frying, and in stir-fries.

Golden Treasure

Capsicum annuum **'Golden Treasure'**

ORIGIN United States

PODS 6–9 in. long, 1.5–2.5 in. wide; pendant, green to golden yellow

PLANT HEIGHT 24–30 in.

HARVEST Midseason, 70–80 days after transplanting

HEAT LEVEL Sweet

Used for salads, roasting, stuffing, frying, and in stir-fries.

Gypsy Hybrid

Capsicum annuum **'Gypsy Hybrid'**

ORIGIN United States

PODS 4–4.5 in. long, 1.5–2 in. wide; pendant, pale yellow to orange red

PLANT HEIGHT 18–24 in.

HARVEST Midseason, 70–80 days after transplanting

HEAT LEVEL Sweet

All-America Selections winner in 1981. Use fresh in salads or as a frying pepper.

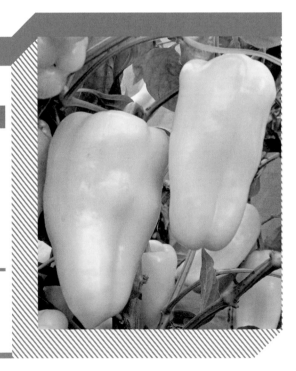

Italia

Capsicum annuum 'Italia'

ORIGIN Italy

PODS 6–8 in. long, 1.5–2.5 in. wide; pendant, green to red

PLANT HEIGHT 18–24 in.

HARVEST Midseason, 70–80 days after transplanting

HEAT LEVEL Sweet

One of the earliest Italian varieties; used for salads, frying, and in stir-fries.

Key Largo Hybrid

Capsicum annuum 'Key Largo Hybrid'

ORIGIN United States

PODS 6–7 in. long, 1.5–2 in. wide; pendant, yellowish green to orange to red

PLANT HEIGHT 24–30 in.

HARVEST Midseason, 70–80 days after transplanting

HEAT LEVEL Sweet

Prolific. Used for salads, frying, and in stir-fries.

Marconi Giant Hybrid

Capsicum annuum 'Marconi Giant Hybrid'

ORIGIN United States

PODS 7–8 in. long, 1.5–2.5 in. wide; pendant, green to red

PLANT HEIGHT 18–24 in.

HARVEST Midseason, 70–80 days after transplanting

HEAT LEVEL Sweet

Resistant to tobacco mosaic virus and Potato virus Y (PVY). Good in salads and salsas, or roasted, grilled, and fried.

Marconi Golden

Capsicum annuum 'Marconi Golden'

ORIGIN Italy

PODS 6–10 in. long, 1.5–2.5 in. wide; pendant, green to golden yellow

PLANT HEIGHT 18–24 in.

HARVEST Midseason, 70–80 days after transplanting

HEAT LEVEL Sweet

Used in Italian cuisine and for grilling, roasting, stuffing, frying, and in stir-fries. Also good when fresh.

Marconi Purple

Capsicum annuum 'Marconi Purple'

ORIGIN Italy

PODS 6–8 in. long, 1.5–2.5 in. wide; pendant, pale green to blackish purple to red

PLANT HEIGHT 18-24 in.

HARVEST Midseason, 70–80 days after transplanting

HEAT LEVEL Sweet

Used in Italian cuisine and for salads, roasting, frying, and in stir-fries.

Marconi Red

Capsicum annuum 'Marconi Red'

ORIGIN Italy

PODS 6–10 in. long, 1.5–2.5 in. wide; pendant, green to red

PLANT HEIGHT 18–24 in.

HARVEST Midseason, 70–80 days after transplanting

HEAT LEVEL Sweet

Used in Italian cuisine and for salads, roasting, frying, and in stir-fries.

Melrose

Capsicum annuum 'Melrose'

ORIGIN Italy

PODS 3.5–4.5 in. long, 1–1.5 in. wide; upright to pendant, green to red

PLANT HEIGHT 18–24 in.

HARVEST Midseason, 70–80 days after transplanting

HEAT LEVEL Sweet

Heirloom, widely grown in the Chicago area. Used in Italian cuisine and for salads, roasting, frying, and in stir-fries.

Nardello

Capsicum annuum 'Nardello'

ORIGIN Italy

PODS 6–10 in. long, 0.75–1.25 in. wide; pendant, green to brown to red

PLANT HEIGHT 18–24 in.

HARVEST Early season, 60–70 days after transplanting

HEAT LEVEL Sweet

From the small village of Ruoti in the Basilicata region of southern Italy, Giuseppe Nardello brought this heirloom to the states, where it was introduced in 1887. Used in Italian cuisine and can be grilled or chopped and sautéed with other vegetables, or used raw in salsas and salads.

Piquillo

Capsicum annuum 'Piquillo'

ORIGIN Spain

PODS 3–3.5 in. long, 1.5–1.75 in. wide; upright to pendant, green to red

PLANT HEIGHT 24–30 in.

HARVEST Midseason, 70–80 days after transplanting

HEAT LEVEL Sweet

Used for stuffing and roasting, or fresh in salads and salsas.

Relleno

Capsicum annuum 'Relleno'

ORIGIN Italy

PODS 5–8 in. long, 0.75–1.25 in. wide; pendant, yellowish green to red

PLANT HEIGHT 18–24 in.

HARVEST Early season, 60–70 days after transplanting

HEAT LEVEL Mild

Dependable variety for cool-season climates. Used for stuffing, roasting, frying, canning, processing, and in stir-fries.

The Godfather Hybrid

Capsicum annuum 'The Godfather Hybrid'

ORIGIN United States

PODS 5–7 in. long, 1–1.5 in. wide; pendant, pale green to red

PLANT HEIGHT 18–24 in.

HARVEST Midseason, 70–80 days after transplanting

HEAT LEVEL Sweet

Prolific. Used in salads and for roasting, frying, and stir-frying.

De Árbol

The name *de árbol* means "treelike," a reference to the woody stems and erect habit of the plant. Mexican common names for this type include *pico de pajaro* ("bird's beak") and *cola de rata* ("rat's tail"). Although a "Chile-de-Arbol" was mentioned by Francisco Hernández in 1615, it does not resemble the type of today. The de árbol type is believed to be derived from the cayenne, and some references list the two types together. In Mexico, however, it is regarded as a separate type and is often called alfilerillo ("little pin") because of consumer preference for the thinnest pods.

The plant has multiple stems, an upright habit, and grows to 3 feet tall. The leaves are lanceolate to ovate, and vary from smooth to very pubescent (hairy) and are green in color. The pods are elongate, pendant, and pointed, measuring 2–3 inches long by ⅜ inch wide. The mature pods are dark red but dry to translucency. Chile de árbol measures between 15,000 and 30,000 SHUs.

About 6000 acres of de árbol are grown in Mexico, primarily along the coast of Nayarit, the high plains of Jalisco, and some parts of Sinaloa, Zacatecas, and Aguascalientes.

In Mexico, lovers of the de árbol variety think that the thinner pods are closest in taste and appearance to the wild, undomesticated pods. The belief that the de árbol was once wild, combined with its small, thin pods and leaves, has led to speculation that this variety may be more closely related to the piquín than the cayenne. Under cultivation, previously wild chile plants tend to develop larger and longer pods.

The de árbol type is usually ground into a dry powder to give a distinctive flavor to red chile sauces. Individual pods are often added to soups and stews to increase the heat levels, and they are often the primary heat source for table sauces, chile oils, and vinegars.

De Árbol

Capsicum annuum 'De Árbol'

ORIGIN Mexico

PODS 2.5–3.5 in. long, 0.25–0.375 in. wide; pendant, green to red

PLANT HEIGHT 18–24 in.

HARVEST Midseason, 70–80 days after transplanting

HEAT LEVEL Very hot

Used in Mexican cuisine and for making sauces.

De Árbol Purple

Capsicum annuum 'De Árbol Purple'

ORIGIN Mexico, United States

PODS 2–3 in. long, 0.25–0.375 in. wide; pendant, green to purple to red

PLANT HEIGHT 18–24 in.

HARVEST Midseason, 70–80 days after transplanting

HEAT LEVEL Hot

Used dried for sauces and ornamental purposes.

European

This is a collection of related pepper varieties from Europe that do not fit easily into other pod types. While there is so much diversity of plant and pod characteristics in this type, most European varieties are compact to semi-erect and grow to 12–18 inches. The leaves are ovate and medium green and smooth. Flower corollas are white with no spots. Pod shape varies greatly, and can be upright or pendant, and round or blocky or pointed. European varieties are suited for cool-season climates, often needing a short growing period of 60–70 days.

Ammazzo

Capsicum annuum **'Ammazzo'**

ORIGIN Italy

PODS 0.5–0.75 in. long, 0.5–0.75 in. wide; upright, dark green to red

PLANT HEIGHT 18–24 in.

HARVEST Midseason, 70–80 days after transplanting

HEAT LEVEL Medium

Cluster type; fruits resemble red marbles in a green bowl. Can be dried and ground into chile powder.

Antohi Romanian

Capsicum annuum **'Antohi Romanian'**

ORIGIN Romania

PODS 3–4 in. long, 2–2.5 in. wide; pendant, pale yellow to red

PLANT HEIGHT 18–24 in.

HARVEST Early season, 60–70 days after transplanting

HEAT LEVEL Sweet

Heirloom. Blocky fruits are early and productive. Used in Romanian and Hungarian cuisine for paprika, frying, and in stir-fries. Can also be used fresh.

Bulgarian Carrot

Capsicum annuum **'Bulgarian Carrot'**

ORIGIN Bulgaria

PODS 3–3.5 in. long, 0.625–0.75 in. wide; pendant, green to orange

PLANT HEIGHT 12–18 in.

HARVEST Early season, 60–70 days after transplanting

HEAT LEVEL Hot

Used in chutneys, fresh salsas, and for pickling.

Chervena Chujski

Capsicum annuum **'Chervena Chujski'**

ORIGIN Bulgaria

PODS 4–6 in. long, 1.5–2 in. wide; pendant, green to brown to bright red

PLANT HEIGHT 24–30 in.

HARVEST Midseason, 70–80 days after transplanting

HEAT LEVEL Sweet

Prolific. Very sweet flesh. Used for roasting or fresh in salads.

Czechoslovakian Black

Capsicum annuum **'Czechoslovakian Black'**

ORIGIN Czech Republic

PODS 2–2.5 in. long, 1–1.25 in. wide; pendant, black to deep red

PLANT HEIGHT 18–24 in.

HARVEST Midseason, 70–80 days after transplanting

HEAT LEVEL Mild

Both an ornamental pepper and a culinary one. The black fruits can be used for dramatic effect in fresh salsas.

Feherozon

Capsicum annuum 'Feherozon'

ORIGIN Hungary

PODS 3–4 in. long, 2.5–3 in. wide; pendant, pale yellow to orange to red

PLANT HEIGHT 12–18 in.

HARVEST Early season, 60–70 days after transplanting

HEAT LEVEL Sweet

Used in Hungarian cuisine for stuffing and pickling. Can be used fresh.

Georgescu Chocolate

Capsicum annuum 'Georgescu Chocolate'

ORIGIN Romania

PODS 3–4 in. long, 2–2.25 in. wide; pendant, green to reddish brown

PLANT HEIGHT 18–24 in.

HARVEST Midseason, 70–80 days after transplanting

HEAT LEVEL Sweet

A sweet brown, blocky-shaped pepper. Used fresh or roasted.

Georgia Flame

Capsicum annuum 'Georgia Flame'

ORIGIN Republic of Georgia

PODS 5–6 in. long, 2–2.25 in. wide; pendant, green to red

PLANT HEIGHT 18–24 in.

HARVEST Midseason, 70–80 days after transplanting

HEAT LEVEL Hot

Prolific. Excellent in fresh salsas, and when roasted, stuffed, or dried.

Hawaiian Sweet Hot

Capsicum annuum 'Hawaiian Sweet Hot'

ORIGIN United States (Hawaii)

PODS 1.5–2 in. long, 0.5–0.625 in. wide; pendant, green to red

PLANT HEIGHT 18–24 in.

HARVEST Midseason, 70–80 days after transplanting

HEAT LEVEL Hot

Used in fresh salsas and chutneys.

Little Dickens

Capsicum annuum 'Little Dickens'

ORIGIN Unknown

PODS 2.5–3.5 in. long, 0.75–1.25 in. long; upright, green to bright orange

PLANT HEIGHT 6–12 in.

HARVEST Early season, 60–70 days after transplanting

HEAT LEVEL Sweet

Prolific. Used fresh and for pickling.

Orozco

Capsicum annuum 'Orozco'

ORIGIN Eastern Europe

PODS 4–6 in. long, 1.5–2 in. wide; pendant, green to bright orange

PLANT HEIGHT 18–24 in.

HARVEST Midseason, 70–80 days after transplanting

HEAT LEVEL Hot

Used in chutneys, fried, or in stir-fries.

Romanian Sweet

Capsicum annuum 'Romanian Sweet'

ORIGIN Romania

PODS 3–4 in. long, 2–3 in. wide; upright to pendant, pale yellow to orange to red

PLANT HEIGHT 12–18 in.

HARVEST Early season, 60–70 days after transplanting

HEAT LEVEL Sweet

Used fresh and for paprika, frying, and in stir-fries.

Sweet Pickle

Capsicum annuum 'Sweet Pickle'

ORIGIN United States

PODS 2–2.5 in. long, 0.5–0.625 in. wide; upright, yellow to purple splotched to orange to red

PLANT HEIGHT 12–18 in.

HARVEST Early season, 60–70 days after transplanting

HEAT LEVEL Sweet

Prolific. Used fresh and for pickling and ornamental purposes.

Szegedi Giant

Capsicum annuum 'Szegedi Giant'

ORIGIN Hungary

PODS 2–4 in. long, 1.5–2 in. wide; pendant, creamy white to orange to red

PLANT HEIGHT 18–24 in.

HARVEST Early season, 60–70 days after transplanting

HEAT LEVEL Sweet

Used in Hungarian cuisine for paprika and chile powder. Can also be used fresh in salsas.

Tequila Sunrise

Capsicum annuum 'Tequila Sunrise'

ORIGIN United States

PODS 3–3.5 in. long, 0.75–1 in. wide; pendant, green to golden orange

PLANT HEIGHT 18–24 in.

HARVEST Early season, 60–70 days after transplanting

HEAT LEVEL Sweet

Used for pickling and in salads.

Yummy Orange

Capsicum annuum 'Yummy Orange'

ORIGIN Unknown

PODS 2–2.5 in. long, 1–1.25 in. wide; pendant, green to orange

PLANT HEIGHT 18–24 in.

HARVEST Midseason, 70–80 days after transplanting

HEAT LEVEL Sweet

Often found in clamshells in the supermarket—and the focus of much conversation—their extra sweet flavor and the fact that they're practically seedless make these good for snacking. Also used in fresh salsas and for stuffing.

Jalapeño

This chile was named after the city of Xalapa in Veracruz, Mexico, though it is no longer commercially grown there. Jalapeños have a compact single stem or upright, multibranched, spreading habit. The leaves are light to dark green. The flower corollas are white with no spots. The pods, which are conical and cylindrical, are pendant and measure about 2–3 inches long and 1 inch wide. They are green (occasionally sunlight will cause purpling), maturing to red, and measure between 2500 and 7000 SHUs. The brown streaks, or "corking," on the pods are desirable in Mexico but not so in the United States, where the pods are often seen as defective.

In Mexico, commercial cultivation measures approximately 40,000 acres in three main agricultural zones: the Lower Papaloapan River Valley in the states of Veracruz and Oaxaca and the area around Delicias, Chihuahua. The latter region grows the American jalapeños, which are processed and exported to the United States. Approximately 60 percent of the Mexican jalapeño crop is used for processing, 20 percent for fresh consumption, and 20 percent in the production of chipotle chiles, or smoked jalapeños. In the United States, approximately 5500 acres is under cultivation, with Texas the leading state for jalapeño production, followed by New Mexico. Home gardeners should remember that US varieties flourish better in semi-arid climates—dry air combined with irrigation. If planted in hot and humid zones in the United States during the summer, the yield of US varieties decreases, so Mexican varieties should be grown instead. The growing period is 70–80 days after transplanting, and the yield is about 25–35 pods per plant.

Among the most famous chile peppers, jalapeños are instantly recognizable and a considerable mythology has sprung up around them, particularly in Texas. The impetus for their popularity comes from a combination of their unique taste, heat, and continued use as a snack food. In 1956, *Newsweek* published a story on a pepper-eating contest held in the Bayou Teche region of Louisiana, near the home of the famous Tabasco sauce. The article rated the jalapeño as "the hottest pepper known," more fiery than the "green tabasco" or "red cayenne." Thus the "Tex-Mex chile," as it's called, was launched as the perfectly pungent pepper for jalapeño-eating contests, which have since proliferated all over the country.

Biker Billy Hybrid

Capsicum annuum **'Biker Billy Hybrid'**

ORIGIN United States

PODS 3–4 in. long, 1.5–2 in. wide; pendant, green to red

PLANT HEIGHT 18–24 in.

HARVEST Midseason, 70–80 days after transplanting

HEAT LEVEL Medium

A prolific hybrid developed by television personality Bill Hufnagle. It can be smoked to make chipotles and stuffed to make hot chiles rellenos, and is also great in fresh salsas.

False Alarm Hybrid

Capsicum annuum **'False Alarm Hybrid'**

ORIGIN United States

PODS 3–3.5 in. long, 1–1.5 in. wide; pendant, green to red

PLANT HEIGHT 18–24 in.

HARVEST Midseason, 70–80 days after transplanting

HEAT LEVEL Mild

A mild form of jalapeño. Used in fresh salsas and for pickling.

Fooled You Hybrid

Capsicum annuum **'Fooled You Hybrid'**

ORIGIN United States

PODS 2.5–3.5 in. long, 1.25–1.75 in. wide; pendant, green to red

PLANT HEIGHT 18–24 in.

HARVEST Midseason, 70–80 days after transplanting

HEAT LEVEL Sweet

A jalapeño with no heat! Used in Mexican cuisine for fresh salsas, pickling, canning, and processing.

Grandpa's Favorite

Capsicum annuum **'Grandpa's Favorite'**

ORIGIN United States

PODS 1–1.5 in. long, 0.5–0.625 in. wide; pendant, green to red

PLANT HEIGHT 12–18 in.

HARVEST Midseason, 70–80 days after transplanting

HEAT LEVEL Medium

Used in fresh salsas. Fruits resemble a miniature jalapeño.

Jalapeño Early

Capsicum annuum **'Jalapeño Early'**

ORIGIN United States

PODS 2–3 in. long, 1–1.5 in. wide; pendant, green to red

PLANT HEIGHT 12–18 in. tall

HARVEST Early season, 60–70 days after transplanting

HEAT LEVEL Medium

This is an earlier maturing variety. Used in Mexican cuisine for fresh salsas, pickling, canning, and processing.

Jalapeño Jumbo

Capsicum annuum 'Jalapeño Jumbo'

ORIGIN Mexico

PODS 2.5–3.5 in. long, 1.25–1.75 in. wide; pendant, green to red

PLANT HEIGHT 18–24 in.

HARVEST Midseason, 70–80 days after transplanting

HEAT LEVEL Medium

Similar to 'NuMex Jalmundo', a jalapeño developed by New Mexico State University, and the large, thick-fleshed 'Mucho Nacho'. The largest jalapeño cultivar, 'Jalapeño Gigante', has pods 5 inches long. All are used in Mexican cuisine for salsas, rellenos, and pickles. Corking on the pods is normal.

Jalapeño M

Capsicum annuum **'Jalapeño M'**

ORIGIN Mexico

PODS 2–3 in. long, 1–1.5 in. wide; pedant, green to red

PLANT HEIGHT 18–24 in.

HARVEST Midseason, 70–80 days after transplanting

HEAT LEVEL Medium

Used in Mexican cuisine for fresh salsas, pickling, canning, and processing. Corking on the pods is normal.

Jalapeño Purple

Capsicum annuum **'Jalapeño Purple'**

ORIGIN United States

PODS 2.5–3 in. long, 1.25–1.75 in. wide; upright to pendant, pale green to purple to red

PLANT HEIGHT 18–24 in.

HARVEST Midseason, 70–80 days after transplanting

HEAT LEVEL Medium

A purple-fruiting jalapeño. Used in Mexican cuisine; makes attractive fresh salsas.

Jalapeño Tam

Capsicum annuum **'Jalapeño Tam'**

ORIGIN United States (Texas)

PODS 2–3 in. long, 1–1.5 in. wide; pendant, green to red

PLANT HEIGHT 18–24 in.

HARVEST Early season, 60–70 days after transplanting

HEAT LEVEL Medium

Used in Mexican cuisine for fresh salsas, pickling, canning, and processing. A slightly milder jalapeño. Developed at Texas A&M University.

Jaloro

Capsicum annuum **'Jaloro'**

ORIGIN United States (Texas)

PODS 2–3 in. long, 1–1.5 in. wide; pendant, pale yellow to orange to red

PLANT HEIGHT 18–24 in. tall

HARVEST Early season, 60–70 days after transplanting

HEAT LEVEL Medium

A yellow jalapeño. Resistant to six viruses. Used in Mexican cuisine for fresh salsas, canning, and processing.

Mitla Hybrid

Capsicum annuum 'Mitla Hybrid'

ORIGIN Mexico

PODS 2–3 in. long, 0.75–1 in. wide; pendant, green to red

PLANT HEIGHT 18–24 in.

HARVEST Early season, 60–70 days after transplanting

HEAT LEVEL Medium

Prolific. Used in Mexican cuisine for fresh salsas, pickling, canning, and processing.

Mucho Nacho Hybrid

Capsicum annuum 'Mucho Nacho Hybrid'

ORIGIN Mexico

PODS 2.5–3.5 in. long, 1–1.25 in. wide; pendant, green to red

PLANT HEIGHT 18–24 in.

HARVEST Midseason, 70–80 days after transplanting

HEAT LEVEL Medium

Prolific. Used in Mexican cuisine for chipotles and fresh salsas.

Señorita Hybrid

Capsicum annuum 'Señorita Hybrid'

ORIGIN United States

PODS 2–3 in. long, 0.75–1 in. wide; pendant, green to red

PLANT HEIGHT 18–24 in.

HARVEST Early season, 60–70 days after transplanting

HEAT LEVEL Mild

Prolific. A mild jalapeño used in Mexican cuisine for fresh salsas, pickling, canning, and processing.

TAM Vera Cruz

Capsicum annuum **'TAM Vera Cruz'**

ORIGIN United States (Texas)

PODS 2–3 in. long, 0.75–1 in. wide; pendant, green to red

PLANT HEIGHT 18–24 in.

HARVEST Midseason, 70–80 days after transplanting

HEAT LEVEL Medium

Developed by Texas A&M University. Prolific; disease resistant. Used in Mexican cuisine for fresh salsas, pickling, canning, and processing.

Mirasol

The name *mirasol* means "looking at the sun," an allusion to the upright pods on some, but not all, mirasol plants. Perhaps the name is more indicative of the tendency of the pods to curl upward, like an elephant's trunk, hence the name *chile trompa*. The type is also called *chile travieso*, or "naughty" chile, although the heat scale does not bear out its supposedly wicked bite. It is likely that the mirasol type was the *chilcoztli* chile first mentioned by Francisco Hernández in 1615. It appears to be a Mexico native, where it is much loved today.

The plant has an intermediate number of stems and an upright habit, although some varieties tend toward a semi-erect and compact habit. They grow to 24–30 inches. The leaves are smooth and medium green in color. The flower corollas are white with no spots. The pods are elongate and pointed, measuring 2–4 inches long and ¾ inches wide; most mature to a dark red color. Despite the name, the pods of some varieties are borne pendant, not upright.

Bahamian

Capsicum annuum **'Bahamian'**

ORIGIN Bahamas

PODS 1.5–2.5 in. long, 0.25–0.5 in. wide; upright, green to red

PLANT HEIGHT 12–18 in.

HARVEST Midseason, 70–80 days after transplanting

HEAT LEVEL Hot

Used fresh in salsas or dried for sauces.

Bermuda Hot

Capsicum annuum 'Bermuda Hot'

ORIGIN Bermuda

PODS 2.5–3 in. long, 1–1.5 in. wide; upright to pendant, pale green to red

PLANT HEIGHT 12–18 in.

HARVEST Early season, 60–70 days after transplanting

HEAT LEVEL Mild

Prolific. Used in fresh salsa and can be pickled.

Cascabel

Capsicum annuum 'Cascabel'

ORIGIN Mexico

PODS 1–1.25 in. long, 1–1.25 in. wide; pendant, green to dark red

PLANT HEIGHT 24–30 in.

HARVEST Midseason, 70–80 days after transplanting

HEAT LEVEL Medium

Used dried and in Mexican cuisine for sauces. *Cascabel* translates to "little bell" or "rattle," as in its dried form the seeds rattle inside the pod.

Chilcostle

Capsicum annuum **'Chilcostle'**

ORIGIN Mexico (Oaxaca)

PODS 5–6 in. long, 1–1.5 in. wide; pendant, green to brownish red to red

PLANT HEIGHT 24–30 in.

HARVEST Midseason, 70–80 days after transplanting

HEAT LEVEL Medium

Used dried in Mexican cuisine and moles.

Chile De Comida

Capsicum annuum **'Chile De Comida'**

ORIGIN Mexico

PODS 2.5–3.5 in. long, 0.75–1 in. wide; pendant, green to brown to red

PLANT HEIGHT 18–24 in.

HARVEST Midseason, 70–80 days after transplanting

HEAT LEVEL Medium

Used in Mexican cuisine for roasting, frying, and in stir-fries. Can also be used fresh in salsas.

Costeño

Capsicum annuum 'Costeño'

ORIGIN Mexico (Oaxaca)

PODS 3–3.5 in. long, 0.625–0.75 in. wide; pendant, green to red

PLANT HEIGHT 18–24 in.

HARVEST Midseason, 70–80 days after transplanting

HEAT LEVEL Hot

Used fresh or dried and in Mexican cuisine for roasting, frying, and in stir-fries.

Costeño Amarillo

Capsicum annuum 'Costeño Amarillo'

ORIGIN Mexico (Oaxaca)

PODS 3–4 in. long, 0.375–0.5 in. wide; pendant, green to golden yellow to deep orange

PLANT HEIGHT 24–30 in.

HARVEST Midseason, 70–80 days after transplanting

HEAT LEVEL Hot

Mostly used in the dried form to give a yellow coloration to sauces, including moles.

De Agua

Capsicum annuum **'De Agua'**

ORIGIN Mexico (Oaxaca)

PODS 3–5 in. long, 1–1.5 in. wide; upright to pendant, green to red

PLANT HEIGHT 12–18 in.

HARVEST Early season, 60–70 days after transplanting

HEAT LEVEL Medium

Prolific. Used fresh or stuffed or as *rajas con queso* (fried peppers with cheese).

Fresno

Capsicum annuum **'Fresno'**

ORIGIN United States (California)

PODS 2–3 in. long, 1–1.25 in. wide; upright to pendant, green to orange to red

PLANT HEIGHT 18–24 in.

HARVEST Early season, 60–70 days after transplanting

HEAT LEVEL Medium

Prolific. Used for fresh salsas.

Goat's Weed

Capsicum annuum 'Goat's Weed'

ORIGIN Venezuela

PODS 2–2.5 in. long, 0.25–0.375 in. wide; upright, green to black to orange to red

PLANT HEIGHT 24–30 in.

HARVEST Very late season, 90 or more days after transplanting

HEAT LEVEL Very hot

A unique-looking plant with white, pubescent leaves. Black pods make an interesting salsa. Can also be used dried.

Mirasol

Capsicum annuum 'Mirasol'

ORIGIN Mexico

PODS 2–3 in. long, 0.5–0.75 in. wide; upright, green to red

PLANT HEIGHT 18–24 in.

HARVEST Midseason, 70–80 days after transplanting

HEAT LEVEL Medium

Used in Mexican cuisine. Known for its pungent flavor with hints of strawberry.

Purira

Capsicum annuum 'Purira'

ORIGIN Probably Mexico

PODS 2–2.5 in. long, 0.5–0.625 in. wide; upright, greenish yellow with purple splotches to yellow to orange to red

PLANT HEIGHT 18–24 in.

HARVEST Midseason, 70–80 days after transplanting

HEAT LEVEL Very hot

A rainbow of colors produces quite spicy pods. Used fresh in salsas.

West Virginia Pea

Capsicum annuum **'West Virginia Pea'**

ORIGIN United States (West Virginia)

PODS 0.5–0.75 in. long, 0.5–0.75 in. wide; upright, green to red

PLANT HEIGHT 18–24 in.

HARVEST Midseason, 70–80 days after transplanting

HEAT LEVEL Hot

Edible, but also used for ornamental purposes like borders and edging. Good container plant.

Yellow Bedder

Capsicum annuum **'Yellow Bedder'**

ORIGIN United States

PODS 2.5–3 in. long, 0.375–0.5 in. wide; upright, green to golden yellow

PLANT HEIGHT 12–18 in.

HARVEST Early season, 60–70 days after transplanting

HEAT LEVEL Hot

Prolific. Slightly sweet flavor. Used fresh or dried.

New Mexican

According to many accounts, chile peppers were introduced into what is now the United States by Capitán General Juan de Oñate, the founder of Santa Fe, New Mexico, in 1598. However, they may have been introduced to the Pueblo Indians of New Mexico by the Antonio de Espejo expedition of 1582–1583. According to one of the members of the expedition, Baltasar de Obregón, "They have no chile, but the natives were given some seed to plant."

After the Spanish began settlement, the cultivation of chile peppers exploded, and soon peppers were grown all over New Mexico. It is likely that many different varieties were cultivated, including early forms of jalapeños, serranos, anchos, and pasillas. But one variety that adapted particularly well to New Mexico was a long green chile that turned red in the fall. Formerly called 'Anaheim' because of its transfer to the more settled California around 1900, the New Mexican chiles were cultivated for hundreds of years in the region with such dedication that several distinct varieties developed. These varieties, or "land races" (cultivars adapted to specific communities), called 'Chimayo' and 'Española', had adapted to particular environments and are still planted today in the same fields they were grown in centuries ago; they constitute a small but distinct part of the tons of pods produced each year in New Mexico.

The plant has a mostly compact habit with an intermediate number of stems, and grows between 20 and 30 inches high. The leaves are ovate, medium green, and fairly smooth. The flower corollas are white with no spots. The pods are pendant, elongate, bluntly pointed, and measure between 2 and 12 inches. They are dark green, maturing to various shades of red. Some ornamentals are yellow or brown. Their heat ranges from quite mild to medium, between 500 and 2500 SHUs. More than 40,000 acres of New Mexican chiles are under cultivation in New Mexico, California, Arizona, and Texas. The growing period is about 80 days after transplanting.

The earliest cultivated chiles in New Mexico were smaller than those of today; indeed, they were (and still are, in some cases) considered a spice. But as the land races developed and the size of the pods increased, the food value of chiles became evident.

There was just one problem: the bewildering sizes and shapes of the chile peppers made it very difficult for farmers to determine which variety of chile they were growing from year to year. And there was no way to tell how large the pods might be, or how hot. The demand for chiles was increasing as the population of the state did, so it was time for modern horticulture to take over. In 1907, Fabian Garcia, a horticulturist at the Agricultural Experiment Station at the College of Agriculture and Mechanical Arts (now New Mexico State University), began his first experiments in breeding more standardized chile varieties, and, in 1908, published "Chile Culture," the first chile bulletin from the Agricultural Experiment Station.

In 1913, Garcia became director of the Experiment Station and expanded his breeding program. Finally, in 1917, after 10 years of experiments with various strains of pasilla chiles, Garcia released 'New Mexico No. 9', the first attempt to grow chiles with a dependable pod size and heat level. The No. 9 variety became the chile standard in New Mexico until 1950, when Roy Harper, another horticulturist, released 'New Mexico No. 6', a variety that matured earlier, produced higher yields, was wilt resistant, and was less pungent than No. 9.

The 'New Mexico No. 6' variety was by far the biggest breakthrough in the chile-breeding program. According to the late Roy Nakayama, who succeeded Harper as director of the New Mexico Agricultural Experiment Station, "The No. 6 variety changed the image of chile from a ball of fire that sent consumers rushing to the water jug to that of a multipurpose vegetable with a pleasing flavor. Commercial production and marketing, especially of green chiles and sauces, have been growing steadily since people around the world have discovered the delicious taste of chile without the overpowering pungency."

In 1957, the 'New Mexico No. 6' variety was modified, made less pungent again, and the new variety was called 'New Mexico

No. 6-4'. The No. 6-4 variety became the chile industry standard in New Mexico and over 30 years later was still the most popular chile commercially grown in the state. Other chile varieties, such as 'Big Jim' (popular with home gardeners) and 'New Mexico R-Naky', have been developed but became popular mostly with home gardeners.

All of the primary dishes in New Mexican cuisine contain chile peppers: sauces, stews, carne adovada, enchiladas, posole, tamales, huevos rancheros, and many combination vegetable dishes. The intense use of chiles as a food rather than just as a spice or condiment is what differentiates New Mexican cuisine from that of Texas or Arizona. In neighboring states, chile powders are used as a seasoning for beef or chicken broth–based "chili gravies," which are thickened with flour or cornstarch before used as a topping for, say, enchiladas. In New Mexico, the sauces are made from pure chiles and are thickened by reducing the crushed or pureed pods.

New Mexican chile sauces are cooked and pureed, while salsas utilize fresh ingredients and are uncooked. Debates rage over whether tomatoes are used in cooked sauces, such as red chile sauce for enchiladas. Despite the recipes in numerous cookbooks, traditional cooked red sauces do *not* contain tomatoes, though uncooked salsas do.

New Mexicans love chile peppers so much that they have become the de facto state symbol. Houses are adorned with strings of dried red chiles, called ristras, and images of the pods are emblazoned on signs, t-shirts, coffee mugs, posters, windsocks, and even underwear. In the late summer and early fall, the aroma of roasting chiles fills the air and produces a state of bliss for chileheads.

"*A la primera cocinera se le va un chile entero,*" goes one old Spanish *dicho*, or saying ("To the best lady cook goes the whole chile"). And the chile pepper is the single most important food brought from Mexico that defines New Mexican cuisine.

Anaheim M

Capsicum annuum **'Anaheim M'**

ORIGIN United States (California)

PODS 6–8 in. long, 1–2 in. wide; pendant, green to red

PLANT HEIGHT 18–24 in.

HARVEST Midseason, 70–80 days after transplanting

HEAT LEVEL Mild

Used for sauces, stuffing, roasting, canning, processing, frying, and in stir-fries.

Anaheim TMR23

Capsicum annuum **'Anaheim TMR23'**

ORIGIN United States (California)

PODS 6–8 in. long, 1–2 in. wide; pendant, green to red

PLANT HEIGHT 18–24 in.

HARVEST Midseason, 70–80 days after transplanting

HEAT LEVEL Medium

Used for sauces, stuffing, roasting, canning, processing, frying, and in stir-fries.

Barker's Hot

Capsicum annuum 'Barker's Hot'

ORIGIN United States (New Mexico)

PODS 5–7 in. long, 1–2 in. wide; pendant, green to red

PLANT HEIGHT 18–24 in.

HARVEST Midseason, 70–80 days after transplanting

HEAT LEVEL Medium

One of the hottest of the New Mexican pod types. Used for sauces, stuffing, roasting, canning, processing, frying, and in stir-fries.

Big Chile Hybrid

Capsicum annuum 'Big Chile Hybrid'

ORIGIN United States

PODS 7–9 in. long, 1–1.5 in. wide; pendant, green to red

PLANT HEIGHT 18–24 in.

HARVEST Midseason, 70–80 days after transplanting

HEAT LEVEL Mild

Prolific. Used for sauces, stuffing, roasting, canning, processing, frying, and in stir-fries.

Big Jim

Capsicum annuum 'Big Jim'

ORIGIN United States (New Mexico)

PODS 6–9 in. long, 1.5–2 in. wide; pendant, green to red

PLANT HEIGHT 18–24 in.

HARVEST Midseason, 70–80 days after transplanting

HEAT LEVEL Medium

One of the largest cultivars among New Mexican pod types. Used for sauces, stuffing, roasting, canning, processing, frying, and in stir-fries.

Chimayó

Capsicum annuum 'Chimayó'

ORIGIN United States (New Mexico)

PODS 3–4 in. long, 1–1.75 in. wide; pendant, green to red

PLANT HEIGHT 12–18 in.

HARVEST Early season, 60–70 days after transplanting

HEAT LEVEL Medium

A land race from the Chimayó area. Used as powder and for fresh salsas and sauces, stuffing, roasting, canning, processing, frying, and in stir-fries.

Cochiti

Capsicum annuum **'Cochiti'**

ORIGIN United States (New Mexico)

PODS 4–5 in. long, 1–1.25 in. wide; pendant, green to red

PLANT HEIGHT 18–24 in.

HARVEST Early season, 60–70 days after transplanting

HEAT LEVEL Medium

A land race from Cochiti Pueblo. Prolific. Used as powder and for fresh salsas and sauces, stuffing, roasting, canning, processing, frying, and in stir-fries.

College 64

Capsicum annuum 'College 64'

ORIGIN United States (New Mexico)

PODS 6–8 in. long, 1–1.5 in. wide; pendant, green to red

PLANT HEIGHT 18–24 in.

HARVEST Early season, 60–70 days after transplanting

HEAT LEVEL Mild

Used as powder and for fresh salsas and sauces, stuffing, roasting, canning, processing, frying, and in stir-fries.

Conquistador

Capsicum annuum 'Conquistador'

ORIGIN United States (New Mexico)

PODS 6–7 in. long, 1–1.5 in. wide; pendant, green to red

PLANT HEIGHT 18–24 in.

HARVEST Midseason, 70–80 days after transplanting

HEAT LEVEL Sweet

Sometimes known as 'Spanish Paprika'. A nonpungent New Mex variety. Used fresh in salsas and for stuffing, roasting, frying, and in stir-fries.

Cow Horn

Capsicum annuum 'Cow Horn'

ORIGIN United States (probably Texas)

PODS 6–8 in. long, 1.25–1.5 in. wide; pendant, green to red, sometimes green to yellow

PLANT HEIGHT 18–24 in.

HARVEST Midseason, 70–80 days after transplanting

HEAT LEVEL Medium

Curved fruit resembles a horn. Used as powder and for fresh salsas and sauces, stuffing, roasting, canning, processing, frying, and in stir-fries.

Crimson Hot

Capsicum annuum **'Crimson Hot'**

ORIGIN United States

PODS 5–7 in. long, 1.25–1.5 in. wide; pendant, green to red

PLANT HEIGHT 18–24 in.

HARVEST Midseason, 70–80 days after transplanting

HEAT LEVEL Medium

Used as powder and for fresh salsas and sauces, stuffing, roasting, canning, processing, frying, and in stir-fries.

Española Improved

Capsicum annuum **'Española Improved'**

ORIGIN United States (New Mexico)

PODS 5–6 in. long, 1–1.5 in. wide; pendant, green to red

PLANT HEIGHT 18–24 in.

HARVEST Early, 60–70 days after transplanting

HEAT LEVEL Medium

Used as powder and for fresh salsas and sauces, stuffing, roasting, canning, processing, frying, and in stir-fries.

Guajillo

Capsicum annuum **'Guajillo'**

ORIGIN Mexico

PODS 4–4.5 in. long, 1–1.25 in. wide; pendant, green to brown to red

PLANT HEIGHT 24–30 in.

HARVEST Midseason, 70–80 days after transplanting

HEAT LEVEL Medium

Used dried and in Mexican cuisine for moles and other sauces, as well as for stuffing, roasting, canning, processing, frying, and in stir-fries. Thought to be one of the forerunners to the New Mexican pod type.

Jemez

Capsicum annuum **'Jemez'**

ORIGIN United States (New Mexico)

PODS 3–5 in. long, 1–1.5 in. wide; pendant, green to red

PLANT HEIGHT 12–18 in.

HARVEST Early season, 60–70 days after transplanting

HEAT LEVEL Medium

Land race from Jemez Pueblo. Used as powder and for fresh salsas and sauces, stuffing, roasting, canning, processing, frying, and in stir-fries.

NuMex 6-4

Capsicum annuum 'NuMex 6-4'

ORIGIN United States (New Mexico)

PODS 5–7 in. long, 1–1.5 in. wide; pendant, green to red

PLANT HEIGHT 24–30 in.

HARVEST Midseason, 70–80 days after transplanting

HEAT LEVEL Mild

A new variety developed from the original germ plasm, 'NuMex 6-4 Improved', is now available from the Chile Pepper Institute. Used as powder and for fresh salsas and sauces, stuffing, roasting, canning, and processing.

NuMex Joe E. Parker

Capsicum annuum 'NuMex Joe E. Parker'

ORIGIN United States (New Mexico)

PODS 6–7 in. long, 1–1.5 in. wide; pendant, green to red

PLANT HEIGHT 24–30 in.

HARVEST Midseason, 70–80 days after transplanting

HEAT LEVEL Mild

Sometimes listed as 'Joe Parker'. Used as powder and for fresh salsas and sauces, stuffing, roasting, canning, processing, frying, and in stir-fries.

NuMex R Naky

Capsicum annuum **'NuMex R Naky'**

ORIGIN United States

PODS 5–6 in. long, 1–1.25 in. wide; pendant, green to red

PLANT HEIGHT 24–30 in.

HARVEST Midseason, 70–80 days after transplanting

HEAT LEVEL Mild

Sometimes listed as 'R Naky'. Named after famed chile breeder Roy Nakayama. Used in sauces for New Mexico chile dishes such as enchiladas. They are also stuffed for chiles rellenos.

NuMex Sandia

Capsicum annuum **'NuMex Sandia'**

ORIGIN United States (New Mexico)

PODS 6–7 in. long; 1–2 in. wide; pendant, green to red

PLANT HEIGHT 24–30 in.

HARVEST Midseason, 70–80 days after transplanting

HEAT LEVEL Hot

Sometimes listed as 'Sandia'. One of the hottest of the New Mexican pod types. Used as powder and for fresh salsas and sauces, stuffing, roasting, canning, and processing.

Ortega

Capsicum annuum 'Ortega'

ORIGIN United States (California)

PODS 6–7 in. long, 1–1.5 in. wide; pendant, green to red

PLANT HEIGHT 24–30 in.

HARVEST Midseason, 70–80 days after transplanting

HEAT LEVEL Mild

Originated from TMR23 stock. Used as powder and for fresh salsas and sauces, stuffing, roasting, canning, and processing.

Pueblo

Capsicum annuum 'Pueblo'

ORIGIN United States (New Mexico)

PODS 5–7 in. long, 1.5–2 in. wide; pendant, green to red

PLANT HEIGHT 24–30 in.

HARVEST Midseason, 70–80 days after transplanting

HEAT LEVEL Mild

Used as powder and for fresh salsas and sauces, stuffing, roasting, canning, and processing.

Slim Jim

Capsicum annuum 'Slim Jim'

ORIGIN United States

PODS 7–9 in. long, 1–1.25 in. wide; pendant, green to red

PLANT HEIGHT 24–30 in.

HARVEST Midseason, 70–80 days after transplanting

HEAT LEVEL Mild

A slimmer pod. Used as powder and for roasting and stuffing, frying, and in stir-fries, as well as for canning and processing.

Ornamental

Although edible, ornamentals are grown primarily for their unusual pod shapes or for their dense foliage and colorful, erect fruits. Many other pod types can be used as ornamentals, such as the piquíns.

Many ornamentals have multiple stems and a compact habit. In low-light situations, some ornamentals adopt a vinelike habit. The flower corollas are white or purple with no spots. The pods vary greatly in shape, from small, piquínlike pods to extremely long and thin cayennelike pods. In between, they can assume nearly any shape imaginable. The pods also vary greatly in heat, ranging from zero to 50,000 SHUs. One distinguishing factor of ornamentals is their ability to live in pots as perennials. In the garden, however, they often grow larger than they do in pots.

Ornamentals are used mostly for decoration, but they can also be pickled or dried.

Aurora

Capsicum annuum 'Aurora'

ORIGIN Unknown

PODS 1.25–1.5 in. long, 0.625–0.75 in. wide; upright, pale green to purple to orange to red

PLANT HEIGHT 6–12 in.

HARVEST Early season, 60–70 days after transplanting

HEAT LEVEL Very hot

Often used for ornamental purposes because of the rainbow of colors on the plant at the same time. Edible; makes a colorful chile vinegar.

Black Prince

Capsicum annuum **'Black Prince'**

ORIGIN United States

PODS 1–1.25 in. long, 0.25–0.5 in. wide; upright, blackish purple to red

PLANT HEIGHT 18–24 in.

HARVEST Midseason, 70–80 days after transplanting

HEAT LEVEL Hot

Edible, but often used for ornamental purposes like borders and edging. Its black leaves and fruits make for a dramatic effect. Good container plant. Keep black-foliaged plants a bit dryer as they don't transpire moisture as quickly as those with green foliage.

Bolivian Rainbow

Capsicum annuum **'Bolivian Rainbow'**

ORIGIN Bolivia

PODS 0.5–0.75 in. long, 0.375–0.5 in. wide; upright, purple to yellow to orange to red

PLANT HEIGHT 18–24 in.

HARVEST Midseason, 70–80 days after transplanting

HEAT LEVEL Hot

Edible, but often used for ornamental purposes like borders and edging. You may see all colors on the plant at once. Good container plant.

Candlelight

Capsicum annuum **'Candlelight'**

ORIGIN United States

PODS 0.75–1.25 in. long, 0.25–0.5 in. wide; upright, green to orange to red

PLANT HEIGHT 6–12 in.

HARVEST Midseason, 70–80 days after transplanting

HEAT LEVEL Very hot

Edible, but often used for ornamental purposes like borders and edging. Compact and pretty; good container plant.

Centennial Rainbow

Capsicum annuum 'Centennial Rainbow'

ORIGIN United States (New Mexico)

PODS 0.5-1 in. long, 0.5-0.625 in. wide; upright, pale yellow to purple splotched to orange to red

PLANT HEIGHT 6-12 in.

HARVEST Midseason, 70-80 days after transplanting

HEAT LEVEL Hot

Edible, but often used for ornamental purposes like borders and edging. Good container plant.

Chilly Chili Hybrid

Capsicum annuum 'Chilly Chili Hybrid'

ORIGIN United States

PODS 2-2.5 in. long, 0.25-0.375 in. wide; upright, greenish yellow to orange to red

PLANT HEIGHT 6-12 in.

HARVEST Midseason, 70-80 days after transplanting

HEAT LEVEL Mild

A child-proof nonpungent variety. Edible, but often used for ornamental purposes like borders and edging. Good container plant.

Chinese Multi-Color

Capsicum annuum **'Chinese Multi-Color'**

ORIGIN China

PODS 1–1.25 in. long, 0.5–0.75 in. wide; upright, purple to cream to yellow to orange to red

PLANT HEIGHT 24–30 in.

HARVEST Midseason, 70–80 days after transplanting

HEAT LEVEL Very hot

A larger piquín in beautiful colors on a taller plant. Edible, but often used for ornamental purposes.

Christmas

Capsicum annuum **'Christmas'**

ORIGIN New Mexico

PODS 1–1.5 in. long, 0.5–0.625 in. wide; upright, creamy white to purple to yellow to orange to red

PLANT HEIGHT 6 to12 in.

HARVEST Midseason, 70–80 days after transplanting

HEAT LEVEL Medium

Also known as 'NuMex Christmas'. Prolific. Edible; sweet flavor. Often used for ornamental purposes.

Color Guard

Capsicum annuum **'Color Guard'**

ORIGIN United States

PODS 1–1.25 in. long, 0.25–0.5 in. wide; upright, pale yellow to purple to orange to red

PLANT HEIGHT 12–18 in.

HARVEST Midseason, 70–80 days after transplanting

HEAT LEVEL Medium

Edible, but mostly used for ornamental purposes like borders and edging.

Ecuador Hot

Capsicum annuum **'Ecuador Hot'**

ORIGIN Ecuador

PODS 0.75–1 in. long, 0.375–0.5 in. wide; pendant, purple to yellow to orange to red

PLANT HEIGHT 24–30 in.

HARVEST Late season, 80–90 days after transplanting

HEAT LEVEL Very hot

Prolific, with green, purple and white leaves. Edible, but used for ornamental purposes like borders and edging. Good container plant.

Filius Blue

Capsicum annuum **'Filius Blue'**

ORIGIN United States

PODS 0.5–0.75 in. long and wide; upright, purple to red

PLANT HEIGHT 6–12 in.

HARVEST Midseason, 70–80 days after transplanting

HEAT LEVEL Hot

Despite its name, the round fruits are more purple than blue. Edible, but used for ornamental purposes like borders and edging. Good container plant.

Fish

Capsicum annuum 'Fish'

ORIGIN United States

PODS 2–2.5 in. long, 0.5–0.625 in. wide; pendant, green with yellow stripes to red with orange stripes

PLANT HEIGHT 18–24 in.

HARVEST Midseason, 70–80 days after transplanting

HEAT LEVEL Hot

An African American heirloom with striped fruits popular in the Philadelphia, PA, and Baltimore, MD, areas. Good container plant.

Five Color

Capsicum annuum 'Five Color'

ORIGIN China

PODS 1–1.25 in. long, 0.5–0.75 in. wide; upright, purple to cream to yellow to orange to red

PLANT HEIGHT 18–24 in.

HARVEST Midseason, 70–80 days after transplanting

HEAT LEVEL Hot

Also known as 'Chinese Five Color'. A real beauty with larger piquín pods in five colors. Edible, but used for ornamental purposes like borders and edging. Good container plant.

Holiday Time

Capsicum annuum 'Holiday Time'

ORIGIN Honduras

PODS 0.5–0.625 in. long and wide; upright, creamy white to purple to yellow to orange to red

PLANT HEIGHT 6–12 in.

HARVEST Midseason, 70–80 days after transplanting

HEAT LEVEL Hot

Pods look like marbles. Edible, but used for ornamental purposes like borders and edging. Good container plant.

Korean Hot

Capsicum annuum 'Korean Hot'

ORIGIN Korea

PODS 0.5–0.75 in. long and wide; upright, creamy white to purple to yellow to orange to red

PLANT HEIGHT 12–18 in.

HARVEST Midseason, 70–80 days after transplanting

HEAT LEVEL Hot

Edible, but used for ornamental purposes like borders and edging. Good container plant.

Little Elf

Capsicum annuum 'Little Elf'

ORIGIN Hungary

PODS 0.75–1 in. long, 0.375–0.5 in. wide; upright, yellow to purple to orange to red

PLANT HEIGHT 6–12 in.

HARVEST Midseason, 70–80 days after transplanting

HEAT LEVEL Medium

Edible, but used for ornamental purposes like borders and edging. Good container plant.

Masquerade

Capsicum annuum 'Masquerade'

ORIGIN United States

PODS 2–3 in. long, 0.25–0.5 in. wide; upright, green to purple to red

PLANT HEIGHT 6–12 in.

HARVEST Midseason, 70–80 days after transplanting

HEAT LEVEL Hot

Edible, but used for ornamental purposes like borders and edging. Good container plant.

Poinsettia

Capsicum annuum 'Poinsettia'

ORIGIN United States

PODS 2.5–3.5 in. long, 0.375–0.5 in. wide; upright, green to red

PLANT HEIGHT 18–24 in.

HARVEST Midseason, 70–80 days after transplanting

HEAT LEVEL Very hot

Edible (used in Asian cuisine), but used for ornamental purposes like borders and edging. Good container plant.

Pretty Purple

Capsicum annuum **'Pretty Purple'**

ORIGIN United States

PODS 0.5–0.75 in. long and wide; upright, purple to red

PLANT HEIGHT 6–12 in.

HARVEST Midseason, 70–80 days after transplanting

HEAT LEVEL Hot

Used for ornamental purposes like borders and edging. Good container plant.

Riot

Capsicum annuum 'Riot'

ORIGIN United States

PODS 2–3 in. long, 0.25–0.375 in. wide; upright, pale yellow to orange to red

PLANT HEIGHT 6–12 in.

HARVEST Early season, 60–70 days after transplanting

HEAT LEVEL Hot

Cluster type. Used for ornamental purposes like borders and edging. Good container plant.

Vietnamese Multi-Color

Capsicum annuum 'Vietnamese Multi-Color'

ORIGIN Vietnam

PODS 0.625–0.75 in. long, 0.5–0.625 in. wide; upright, purple to cream to yellow to orange to red

PLANT HEIGHT 18–24 in.

HARVEST Midseason, 70–80 days after transplanting

HEAT LEVEL Medium

Edible, but used for ornamental purposes like borders and edging. Good container plant.

Paprika

The word *paprika* derives from the Hungarian *paparka*, which is a variation on the Bulgarian *piperka*, which in turn was derived from the Latin *piper*, for "pepper." In the United States, the *paprika* simply means any nonpungent red chile, mostly New Mexican pod types that have had their pungency removed by traditional breeding. In Europe, however, paprika has much greater depth, having not only distinct pod types but also specific grades of the powders made from these pod types.

Sometime between 1538 and 1548, chiles were introduced into Hungary, and the first citizens to accept the fiery pods were the servants and shepherds who had more contact with the Turkish invaders. Author Zoltan Halasz tells the tale: "Hungarian herdsmen started to sprinkle tasty slices of bacon with Paprika and season the savoury stews they cooked in cauldrons over an open fire with the red spice. They were followed by the fishermen of the Danube . . . who would render their fish-dishes more palatable with the red spice, and at last the Hungarian peasantry, consuming with great gusto the meat of fattened oxen and pigs or tender poultry which were prepared in Paprika-gravy, professed their irrevocable addiction to Paprika, which by then had become a characteristically Hungarian condiment."

The famous "Hungarian flavor," which is unique to the cuisine of that country, is created by the combination of lard, paprika, and spices. Chopped onions are always cooked to translucency in the lard; paprika and sour cream are added to pan drippings after meats have been browned to make a rich sauce, which is then served over meat and peppers. There are many versions of hot and spicy recipes with the generic terms of *gulyas* ("goulash") and *paprikas* ("paprikash").

The great pepper-growing areas around Kalocsa and Szeged in Hungary have just the right combination of soil characteristics, temperature, rainfall, and sunshine required to cultivate these plants successfully. In March, the pepper seeds are put in water to germinate, then transferred to greenhouse beds. Seven weeks later, in May, the small pepper shrubs are replanted in the open fields. Harvesting starts at the end of the first week in September and lasts for about a month, depending on weather conditions. By harvest time, the mature plants will have grown to a height of 18–24 inches and the pepper pods—3–5 inches long and about 1–1.5 inches wide—will have ripened from green or yellow to bright red.

In the Hungarian countryside, paprika peppers are threaded onto strings and are hung from the walls, porches, and eaves of farmhouses, much like the chile ristras in the American Southwest. Today Hungary produces both pungent and sweet paprikas, but originally all Hungarian paprika was aromatic and quite hot. It was evidently too hot for some tastes, for by the turn of this century other countries were requesting that Hungary develop a nonpungent variety. By accident, farmers produced a sweet variety in their fields when they planted milder "eating" paprika with hotter "seasoning" paprika nearby, and insects cross-pollinated the two. The resulting hybrid reduced the pungency of the paprika pods and probably led to the nonpungent varieties now grown in Spain.

Food authority Craig Claiborne has noted, "The innocuous powder which most merchants pass on to their customers as paprika has slightly more character than crayon or chalk. Any paprika worthy of its name has an exquisite taste and varies in strength from decidedly hot to pleasantly mild but with a pronounced flavor."

Alma Paprika

Capsicum annuum 'Alma Paprika'

ORIGIN Hungary

PODS 1.5–2 in. long, 1.75–2.25 in. wide; upright, yellow to orange to red

PLANT HEIGHT 12–18 in.

HARVEST Early season, 60–70 days after transplanting

HEAT LEVEL Medium

Crunchy, with lingering sweet heat. Used in Hungarian cuisine and for paprika and stuffing.

Boldog Hungarian Spice

Capsicum annuum 'Boldog Hungarian Spice'

ORIGIN Hungary

PODS 4–5 in. long, 1–1.5 in. wide; pendant, green to red

PLANT HEIGHT 18–24 in.

HARVEST Midseason, 70–80 days after transplanting

HEAT LEVEL Mild

Used in Hungarian cuisine and for paprika and chile powder.

Cyklon

Capsicum annuum **'Cyklon'**

ORIGIN Poland

PODS 3.5–4 in. long, 1–1.5 in. wide; pendant, green to red

PLANT HEIGHT 18–24 in.

HARVEST Midseason, 70–80 days after transplanting

HEAT LEVEL Hot

Best dried. Used in Hungarian cuisine and for paprika and spicy chile powder.

Kalocsa Paprika

Capsicum annuum 'Kalocsa Paprika'

ORIGIN Hungary

PODS 4–5 in. long, 1–1.25 in. wide; pendant, green to brown to red

PLANT HEIGHT 18–24 in.

HARVEST Midseason, 70–80 days after transplanting

HEAT LEVEL Mild

Typically used dried in Hungarian cuisine and for paprika and chile powder.

PCR Paprika

Capsicum annuum 'PCR Paprika'

ORIGIN Eastern Europe

PODS 3–4 in. long, 2–3 in. wide; pendant, pale yellow to orange to red

PLANT HEIGHT 18–24 in.

HARVEST Early season, 60–70 days after transplanting

HEAT LEVEL Sweet

Typically used dried in Hungarian cuisine and for paprika and chile powder.

Pasilla

In Spanish, *pasilla* means "little raisin," an allusion to the aroma of the dark brown pods of this type. In California, the ancho is sometimes called pasilla, causing much confusion. In western Mexico, it is sometimes called *chile negro*, a term that also refers to the darker anchos. In the fresh form, the pod is known as chilaca.

The plant has an intermediate number of stems, an erect habit, and grows 2–3 feet high or more. The primary branches begin over 5 inches from the lowest stem portion so the pods will not touch the ground. The leaves are ovate, smooth, and medium green in color. The flowers have white corollas with no spots. The pods are extremely elongate, cylindrical, furrowed, and measure 6 inches long (or more) by 1 inch wide.

Immature fruits are dark green, maturing to dark brown. The growing period is 90–100 days after transplanting. This type is not particularly pungent, measuring between 1000 and 1500 SHUs.

It is likely that the pasilla is the immediate predecessor of the New Mexican type. It has adapted particularly well to the temperate regions of Mexico. About 7500 acres of pasillas are cultivated in Mexico, primarily in Aguascalientes, Jalisco, Zacatecas, and Guanajuato. The annual yield is approximately 3500 tons of dried pods. The most popular Mexican varieties are 'Pabellon One' and 'Apaseo'. There is no commercial US production. The pasilla does well in the home garden, and the pods should be allowed to dry on the plant.

The pasilla is part of the legend of the origin of mole sauces, which also contain other varieties as well. Because it is very flavorful, the pasilla is a favorite of Mexican *moleros*, cooks who specialize in preparing unique mole sauces. The pasilla is mainly used in the dried pod or powder form in sauces such as adobo. It adds an interesting taste and color to standard red chile enchilada sauce as well.

Holy Mole Hybrid

Capsicum annuum 'Holy Mole Hybrid'

ORIGIN United States

PODS 5–7 in. long, 0.75–1 in. wide; pendant, dark green to deep brown

PLANT HEIGHT 30–36 in.

HARVEST Midseason, 70–80 days after transplanting

HEAT LEVEL Mild

A hybid pasilla type and a 2007 All American Selection. Typically used dried. Used in Mexican cuisine and for moles and chile powder.

Pasilla Apaseo

Capsicum annuum 'Pasilla Apaseo'

ORIGIN Mexico

PODS 5–6 in. long, 0.75–1.25 in. wide; pendant, dark green to brown

PLANT HEIGHT 18–24 in.

HARVEST Midseason, 70–80 days after transplanting

HEAT LEVEL Mild

Distinctive flavor; typically used dried. Used in Mexican cuisine and for moles and chile powder.

Pasilla Bajío

Capsicum annuum **'Pasilla Bajío'**

ORIGIN Mexico

PODS 5–7 in. long, 0.75–1 in. wide; pendant, dark green to brown

PLANT HEIGHT 24–30 in.

HARVEST Midseason, 70–80 days after transplanting

HEAT LEVEL Mild

Resistant to tobacco mosaic virus. Distinctive flavor; typically used dried. Used in Mexican cuisine and for moles and chile powder.

Pasilla De Oaxaca

Capsicum annuum **'Pasilla De Oaxaca'**

ORIGIN Oaxaca, Mexico

PODS 5–7 in. long, 0.75–1.25 in. wide; pendant, dark green to brown

PLANT HEIGHT 24–30 in.

HARVEST Midseason, 70–80 days after transplanting

HEAT LEVEL Mild

Used in Mexican cuisine and for moles and chile powder. Typically used dried.

Peperoncini

Peperoncino simply means "chile pepper" in Italian, so varieties of the peperoncini pod type are considered to be of Italian origin no matter where they're now grown. *Peperoncini* is the plural.

Chile peppers first appeared in Italy in 1526, probably transferred from North Africa to Sicily. Their influence on Italian food was only significant in the south until the last 20 years or so. Nowadays, Italian chileheads grow all kinds of chile peppers all over the country.

Most peperoncini types have an erect, multibranching habit with intermediate to multiple stems. The plant grows 18–24 inches, with medium green ovate to lanceolate leaves. Flower corollas are white with no spots. Pods are 3–5 inches long and ripen to red in 70 days, but are often pickled in their immature green stage.

In southern Italy, cayenne-type chiles are commonly combined with tomatoes to make sauces for pasta dishes. Chile is regarded as a spice to be added to taste and to raise the heat level by the individual chef; thus, southern Italian cuisine does not have the reputation of being particularly fiery because such recipes rarely appear in cookbooks. However, lurking beneath the surface of tomato-dominated sauces, as natives of such towns as Bari will attest, is a tradition of extremely pungent chiles. In the Catanzaro region of Calabria, a favorite dish is morseddu, pig or calf livers and hearts seasoned with tomatoes and hot red chiles and served on bread.

Friggitello

Capsicum annuum 'Friggitello'

ORIGIN Italy

PODS 3–4 in. long, 0.75–1 in. wide; pendant, green to red

PLANT HEIGHT 18–24 in.

HARVEST Early season, 60–70 days after transplanting

HEAT LEVEL Sweet

Used dried or in fresh salsas; good for pickling, frying, and in stir-fries.

Golden Greek

Capsicum annuum 'Golden Greek'

ORIGIN Greece, Italy

PODS 4–5 in. long, 1–1.25 in. wide; pendant, yellowish green to red

PLANT HEIGHT 18–24 in.

HARVEST Midseason, 70–80 days after transplanting

HEAT LEVEL Mild

A favorite peperoncini used for pickling and eaten with salads and sandwiches.

Lombardo

Capsicum annuum 'Lombardo'

ORIGIN Italy

PODS 5–6 in. long, 0.75–1 in. wide; pendant, pale green to red

PLANT HEIGHT 18–24 in.

HARVEST Midseason, 70–80 days after transplanting

HEAT LEVEL Sweet

Used dried, and for pickling, frying, and in stir-fries and fresh salsas.

Peperoncini

Capsicum annuum 'Peperoncini'

ORIGIN Italy

PODS 3–4 in. long, 0.75–1 in. long; pendant, green to red

PLANT HEIGHT 24–30 in.

HARVEST Early season, 60–70 days after transplanting

HEAT LEVEL Mild

Yes, chile pepper nomenclature does it again! Here is a variety that is also a generic term. Used in Italian cuisine and for pickling (usually picked and pickled in its immature green stage).

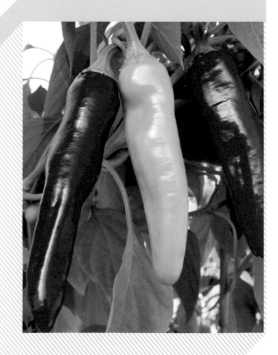

Sigaretto di Bergamo

Capsicum annuum 'Sigaretto di Bergamo'

ORIGIN Italy

PODS 3.5–4.5 in. long, 0.5–0.625 in. wide; pendant, green to brown to red

PLANT HEIGHT 18–24 in.

HARVEST Midseason, 70–80 days after transplanting

HEAT LEVEL Sweet

Also known as 'Cigarette Pepper'. Used for frying, pickles, and in stir-fries.

Pimiento

Pimiento, often Anglicized as "pimento," is characterized by very thick-walled fruit that is green when immature and red at maturity. Fruits have no heat, with pod flesh sweeter than bell peppers. The peppers used for stuffing olives are found in this type, with either heart-shaped or scalloped-edged fruits (also called cheese or tomato peppers). Pimientos are used in processed foods, such as pimiento cheese, but they can also be eaten fresh. Allspice, *Pimiento dioica*, usually known as pimento or Jamaican pepper outside the United States, is not related to *Capsicum*.

The plant is multistemmed with a habit that is subcompact toward prostrate, growing to 18–24 inches. The leaves are medium green, ovate to lanceolate, and smooth. Heart-shaped pods are 3–4 inches long and 1–1½ inches wide. Scalloped-edged pods are round and flattened and 1½ inches long and 3–4 inches wide.

Aleppo

Capsicum annuum 'Aleppo'

ORIGIN Syria

PODS 3.5–4 in. long, 1–1.5 in. wide; pendant, green to red

PLANT HEIGHT 24–30 in.

HARVEST Midseason, 70–80 days after transplanting

HEAT LEVEL Mild

Sometimes known as the halaby pepper, this variety is usually dried and ground into powder.

Apple

Capsicum annuum 'Apple'

ORIGIN Europe

PODS 3–4 in. long, 1.25–2 in. wide; pendant, green to deep red

PLANT HEIGHT 18–24 in.

HARVEST Midseason, 70–80 days after transplanting

HEAT LEVEL Sweet

Can be fried and used in salads or as a garnish; also used to stuff olives.

Figaro

Capsicum annuum 'Figaro'

ORIGIN Italy

PODS 1.5–2 in. long, 2.5–3.5 in. wide; upright becoming pendant, green to bright red

PLANT HEIGHT 18–24 in.

HARVEST Midseason, 70–80 days after transplanting

HEAT LEVEL Sweet

Heirloom; scallop-edged fruits. Used in Italian cuisine and to stuff olives.

Lipstick

Capsicum annuum 'Lipstick'

ORIGIN Europe

PODS 3–4 in. long, 1.5–1.75 in. wide; upright to pendant, green to red

PLANT HEIGHT 18–24 in.

HARVEST Midseason, 70–80 days after transplanting

HEAT LEVEL Sweet

Appears in many specialty markets, where it is considered by customers to be one of the best sweet peppers for salads, salsas, and cooking.

Pimiento de Padrón

Capsicum annuum 'Pimiento de Padrón'

ORIGIN Spain

PODS 2.5–3.5 in. long, 0.75–1.25 in. wide; pendant, green to red

PLANT HEIGHT 18–24 in.

HARVEST Early season, 60–70 days after transplanting

HEAT LEVEL Medium

Heirloom; often called chile pepper roulette because some of the pods in a batch are hot, some not. Used for frying and in stir-fries, usually in its immature stage as the pods get spicier when mature.

Pimiento L

Capsicum annuum 'Pimiento L'

ORIGIN Europe

PODS 3.5–4.5 in. long, 2–3 in. wide; pendant, green to red

PLANT HEIGHT 18–24 in.

HARVEST Midseason, 70–80 days after transplanting

HEAT LEVEL Sweet

Resistant to tobacco mosaic virus. Used fresh, fried, or to stuff olives.

Red Ruffled Pimiento

Capsicum annuum 'Red Ruffled Pimiento

ORIGIN Unknown

PODS 1.5–2 in. long, 3–3.5 in. wide; upright to pendant, green to red

PLANT HEIGHT 18–24 in.

HARVEST Midseason, 70–80 days after transplanting

HEAT LEVEL Sweet

Fruits have scalloped edges. Usually stuffed and fried.

Sheepnose Pimiento

Capsicum annuum **'Sheepnose Pimiento'**

ORIGIN United States (Ohio)

PODS 2–3 in. long, 3–4 in. wide; pendant, green to red

PLANT HEIGHT 18–24 in.

HARVEST Early season, 60–70 days after transplanting

HEAT LEVEL Sweet

Heirloom. Used for stuffing, canning, and processing.

Tennessee Cheese

Capsicum annuum **'Tennessee Cheese'**

ORIGIN United States (Tennessee)

PODS 1–1.75 in. long, 2.5–3.5 in. wide; upright to pendant, green to red

PLANT HEIGHT 18–24 in.

HARVEST Early season, 60–70 days after transplanting

HEAT LEVEL Sweet

Originally from Spain, this cultivar has scalloped-edged fruit. Used for stuffing.

Urfa Biber

Capsicum annuum 'Urfa Biber'

ORIGIN Turkey

PODS 4–6 in. long, 1.5–2 in. wide; pendant, green to red

PLANT HEIGHT 24–30 in.

HARVEST Midseason, 70–80 days after transplanting

HEAT LEVEL Mild

Sometimes known as 'Isot Pepper', this variety is grown in the Urfa region of Turkey. Used for stuffing and chile powder.

Yellow Cheese

Capsicum annuum 'Yellow Cheese'

ORIGIN Unknown

PODS 1–1.5 in. long, 2.5–3.5 in. wide; upright to pendant, green to golden yellow

PLANT HEIGHT 18–24 in.

HARVEST Early season, 60–70 days after transplanting

HEAT LEVEL Sweet

Delicious on their own, these can be used for salsas, canning, or pickling—you can even hollow the scallop-edged fruits out and use them as bowls for individual dip cups.

Piquín

The word *piquín*, also spelled *pequín*, is probably derived from the Spanish *pequeño*, meaning small, an obvious allusion to the size of the fruits. Variations on this form place the words *chile* or *chili* before or in combination with both pequín and tepin forms. The wild form of the piquín type is variously called chiltepín or chilipiquín and it is possible that the word *chilipiquín* is derived from the Náhuatl (Aztec) word *chiltecpín* rather than from *pequeño*.

The piquíns are also known by common names such as bird pepper and chile mosquito. Most are unnamed varieties, both wild and domesticated, varying in pod size and shape from pellets to de árbol–like fruits. Generally speaking, the wild varieties (spherical tepins) are called chiltepíns and the domesticated varieties (oblong piquíns) are called piquíns or pequíns, but in Texas the wild varieties are called chilipiquíns.

Piquíns vary greatly, usually having an intermediate number of stems and an erect habit. In the wild, piquíns can grow 6 feet high or more, and in the greenhouse they have grown 15 feet high in one season. However, some varieties have a prostrate habit, spreading out like a groundcover. The leaves are medium green and lanceolate or ovate. The flower corollas are white with no spots. The pods are borne erect, are round or oblong, and measure between a quarter- and a half-inch long and wide. Domesticated varieties usually have elongate, pointed pods, borne erect but occasionally pendant, sometimes measuring up to 2 inches long. Piquíns are extremely hot, measuring between 50,000 and 100,000 SHUs. In Mexico, the heat of the chiltepín is called *arrebatado* ("rapid," or "violent"), which implies that although the heat is great, it diminishes quickly.

Piquíns were part of the prehistoric migration of *Capsicum annuum* from a nuclear area in southern Brazil or Boliva north to Central America and Mexico. Ethnobotanists believe that birds were responsible for the spread of most wild chiles—indeed, the chiltepín is called the bird pepper. Attempts at domestication of the wild plants have led to the development of the commercial chile piquín, which grows under cultivation in Mexico and Texas (some wild forms have escaped). A cultivated form of the chiltepín has been grown successfully in Sonora and in the Mesilla Valley of New Mexico, where they are planted as annuals. In all cases of domestication, the cultivated forms tend to develop fruits larger than the wild varieties; botanists are not certain whether this trait is the result of better cultural techniques or the natural tendency for humans to pick the largest fruits, which contain next year's seed.

In Mexico, a number of different varieties of piquíns grow wild in the mountains along both coasts: from Sonora to Chiapas on the Pacific and Tamaulipas to Yucatán on the Gulf. They are collected and sold as fresh green, dried red, and in salsas, but the amount of total production is unknown. Some Mexican food companies bottled the chiltepíns *en escabeche* and sell them in supermarkets. In the United States, retail prices for wild chiltepíns reached $48 per pound in 1988.

About a thousand US acres of "small chili" are cultivated, mostly in Texas and New Mexico. Many of these chiles are packaged and labeled as piquín regardless of the shape of their pods—from those resembling red peppercorns to those that look like small New Mexican varieties—and there is no way to tell which are cultivated and which are collected in the wild.

Piquíns do well in the home garden and are particularly suited to being grown in containers as perennials. Garden writer Paul Bessey of the *Arizona Daily Star* reports that rosy-headed house finches regularly decimate his ripening chiltepíns, so some netting protection from birds may be necessary when growing this variety. The growing period is at least 90 days after transplanting.

Popular folklore holds that Texans love chile piquíns so much they eat them right off the bush. In fact, their infatuation is so great that piquín-heads rarely travel far from home without an emergency ration of the tiny pods, either whole or crushed, in a silver snuffbox or pillbox. Texans also reputedly use the chile piquín in place of soap to punish children for using "cuss words."

In 1794, Padre Ignaz Pfefferkorn, an early observer of Sonoran culinary customs, described how the chiltepín (and piquín) was primarily used: "It is placed unpulverized on the table in a salt cellar, and each fancier takes as much of it as he believes he can eat. He pulverizes it with his fingers and mixes it with his food. The chiltepín is still the best spice for soup, boiled peas, lentils, beans, and the like." Today the piquíns and red dried chiltepíns are used precisely the same way, crushed into soups, stews, and bean dishes. The green fruit is chopped and used in salsas and bottled *en escabeche*.

African Pequín

Capsicum annuum 'African Pequin'

ORIGIN Africa

PODS 0.5–0.75 in. long, 0.375–0.5 in. wide; pendant, green to red

PLANT HEIGHT 24–30 in.

HARVEST Very late season, 90 or more days after transplanting

HEAT LEVEL Hot

Prolific. Used dried.

Bailey Piquín

Capsicum annuum 'Bailey Piquín'

ORIGIN United States (New Mexico)

PODS 0.5–0.75 in. long, 0.375–0.5 in. wide; upright, green to red

PLANT HEIGHT 24–30 in.

HARVEST Very late season, 90 or more days after transplanting

HEAT LEVEL Very hot

Also known as 'NuMex Bailey Piquín'; an improved piquín variety. Used dried and crushed into soups and stews.

Bird Dung

Capsicum annuum 'Bird Dung'

ORIGIN Unknown

PODS 0.375–0.5 in. long and wide; upright, green to red

PLANT HEIGHT 18–24 in.

HARVEST Midseason, 70–80 days after transplanting

HEAT LEVEL Hot

Prolific. Used dried and crushed into soups and stews.

Black Cuban

Capsicum annuum **'Black Cuban'**

ORIGIN Cuba

PODS 1.25–1.5 in. long, 0.375–0.5 in. wide; upright, blackish purple to red

PLANT HEIGHT 18–24 in.

HARVEST Midseason, 70–80 days after transplanting

HEAT LEVEL Hot

Used for ornamental purposes; good container plant with dark purple leaves.

Chiltepín

Capsicum annuum 'Chiltepín'

ORIGIN United States, Mexico

PODS 0.25–0.375 in. long and wide; upright, green to red

PLANT HEIGHT 18–24 in.

HARVEST Very late season, 90 or more days after transplanting

HEAT LEVEL Very hot

Used dried to add spice to almost anything; especially effective crushed into soups and stews.

Chiltepín Amarillo

Capsicum annuum 'Chiltepín Amarillo'

ORIGIN Mexico

PODS 0.25–0.375 in. long and wide; upright, green to black to golden yellow

PLANT HEIGHT 18 to 24 in.

HARVEST Very late season, 90 or more days after transplanting

HEAT LEVEL Very hot

A yellow-maturing chiltepín. Used dried to add spice to almost anything; especially effective crushed into soups and stews.

Chiltepín Fort Prescott

Capsicum annuum 'Chiltepín Fort Prescott'

ORIGIN United States (Arizona)

PODS 0.25–0.375 in. long and wide; upright, green to black to red

PLANT HEIGHT 18–24 in.

HARVEST Very late season, 90 or more days after transplanting

HEAT LEVEL Very hot

A wild cultivar found near Prescott, Arizona. Used dried to add spice to almost anything; especially effective crushed into soups and stews.

Chiltepín McMahon's Bird

Capsicum annuum 'Chiltepín McMahon's Bird'

ORIGIN United States (Texas)

PODS 0.25–0.375 in. long and wide; upright, green to red

PLANT HEIGHT 12–18 in.

HARVEST Very late season, 90 or more days after transplanting

HEAT LEVEL Very hot

Used dried to add spice to almost anything; especially effective crushed into soups and stews. A good variety for cool-season gardeners.

Chiltepín Pima Bajo

Capsicum annuum **'Chiltepín Pima Bajo'**

ORIGIN Mexico

PODS 0.25–0.375 in. long and wide; upright, green to black to red

PLANT HEIGHT 18–24 in.

HARVEST Very late season, 90 or more days after transplanting

HEAT LEVEL Very hot

A wild cultivar collected from near the Rio Yaqui. Used dried to add spice to almost anything; especially effective crushed into soups and stews.

Chiltepín Tarahumara

Capsicum annuum **'Chiltepín Tarahumara'**

ORIGIN Mexico

PODS 0.25–0.375 in. long and wide; upright, green to red

PLANT HEIGHT 18–24 in.

HARVEST Very late season, 90 or more days after transplanting

HEAT LEVEL Very hot

A wild cultivar collected from near Sierra Madre in Chihuahua. Used dried to add spice to almost anything; especially effective crushed into soups and stews.

Chiltepín Texas

Capsicum annuum 'Chiltepín Texas'

ORIGIN United States (Texas)

PODS 0.25–0.375 in. long, 0.25–0.375 in. wide; upright, green to red

PLANT HEIGHT 18–24 in.

HARVEST Very late season, 90 or more days after transplanting

HEAT LEVEL Very hot

A wild cultivar collected from near Wimberly, Texas. A good chiltepín for gardens in cool-season climates; an earlier producer. Used dried to add spice to almost anything; especially effective crushed into soups and stews.

Chinese

Capsicum annuum 'Chinese'

ORIGIN China

PODS 0.75–1.25 in. long, 0.25–0.375 in. wide; upright, green to red

PLANT HEIGHT 6–12 in.

HARVEST Midseason, 70–80 days after transplanting

HEAT LEVEL Medium

Prolific. Edible (used in Sichuan and Asian cuisine), but used for ornamental purposes like borders and edging. Good container plant.

Chintexle

Capsicum annuum **'Chintexle'**

ORIGIN Mexico (Oaxaca)

PODS 0.75–1 in. long, 0.375–0.5 in. wide; upright, green to red

PLANT HEIGHT 18–24 in.

HARVEST Midseason, 70–80 days after transplanting

HEAT LEVEL Medium

Used dried in Mexican cuisine; also great roasted over rice dishes.

Cobincho

Capsicum exile **'Cobincho'**

ORIGIN South America

PODS 0.375–0.5 in. long, 0.125–0.25 in. wide; upright, green to orange to red

PLANT HEIGHT 18–24 in.

HARVEST Midseason, 70–80 days after transplanting

HEAT LEVEL Hot

This is a domesticated version of a wild chile sometimes listed as *Capsicum chacoense*. Used to make chile powder, or whole pods can be used to add spice to soups and stews (take the pods out before serving).

Hermosillo

Capsicum annuum 'Hermosillo'

ORIGIN Mexico (Hermosillo, Sonora)

PODS 0.375–0.5 in. long and wide; upright, green to red

PLANT HEIGHT 30–36 in.

HARVEST Very late season, 90 or more days after transplanting

HEAT LEVEL Very hot

Used dried as a spice.

South African Pequín

Capsicum annuum 'South African Pequin'

ORIGIN South Africa

PODS 0.625–0.75 in. long, 0.5–0.625 in. wide; upright, green to red

PLANT HEIGHT 30–36 in.

HARVEST Late season, 80–90 days after transplanting

HEAT LEVEL Hot

Used dried for chile powder and in sauces.

Sport

Capsicum annuum 'Sport'

ORIGIN United States

PODS 1.5–2 in. long, upright; width, 0.375–0.5 in. wide; upright, green to red

PLANT HEIGHT 18–24 in.

HARVEST Midseason, 70–80 days after transplanting

HEAT LEVEL Medium

Prolific. Popular variety in the Chicago area, used in the pickled green stage on hot dogs and sandwiches.

Super Chili Hybrid

Capsicum annuum 'Super Chili Hybrid'

ORIGIN United States

PODS 2–2.5 in. long, 0.375–0.5 in. wide; upright, pale green to orange to red

PLANT HEIGHT 12–18 in.

HARVEST Early season, 60–70 days after transplanting

HEAT LEVEL Hot

Prolific. Used in fresh salsas.

Tabasco Short Yellow

Capsicum annuum 'Tabasco Short Yellow'

ORIGIN United States

PODS 1–1.5 in. long, 0.25–0.375 in. wide; pendant, yellow-green to red

PLANT HEIGHT 24–30 in.

HARVEST Midseason, 70–80 days after transplanting

HEAT LEVEL Hot

Despite the misleading name, this is a *C. annuum* piquín. Used to make hot sauce.

Thai Hot Ornamental

Capsicum annuum 'Thai Hot Ornamental'

ORIGIN Thailand

PODS 0.75–1 inch, 0.25–0.375 in. wide; upright, green to red

PLANT HEIGHT 12–18 in.

HARVEST Midseason, 70–80 days after transplanting

HEAT LEVEL Very hot

Used dried, for ornamental purposes, and in Asian cuisine, such as in stir-fries.

Serrano

In Spanish, *serrano* is an adjective that means "from the mountains." The chile described by this adjective was first grown in the mountains of northern Puebla and Hidalgo, Mexico.

Serranos vary in habit from compact to erect, have an intermediate number of stems, and grow from 1½–5 feet tall. The leaves vary from light to dark green, are pubescent (hairy). The flower corollas are white with no spots. The pods grow pendant, are bluntly pointed, and measure between 1 and 4 inches long and ½ inch wide. Serranos measure between 10,000 and 20,000 SHUs.

Mexico has about 37,500 acres of serranos under cultivation, compared to only 150 acres in the United States, mostly in the Southwest. The states of Veracruz, Sinaloa, Nayarit, and Tamaulipas are the biggest producers of Mexican serrano chiles, growing about 180,000 tons of pods a year. Despite the proliferation of canned serranos, only 10 percent of the crop is processed. The vast majority is used fresh. A very small amount of red serranos is dried out for sale in markets. In 1985, the Texas Agricultural Experiment Station released 'Hidalgo', a mild, multiple virus–resistant strain that is now popular in the United States.

Relatively unknown in the United States until a couple of decades ago, serranos have gained fame because of their pickling. Many different brands of serranos *en escabeche*, or serranos pickled with carrots and onions, have gained favor in the Southwest, where they are consumed as a snack or hors d'ouevre. By far, the most common use of serranos is in fresh salsas. The chiles can be picked fresh from the garden (or from your grocery store), minced, and then combined with a variety of vegetables. The resulting salsas can be used as dips or as condiments for meats, poultry, seafood, and egg dishes.

Fire

Capsicum annuum 'Fire'

ORIGIN Unknown

PODS 2–2.5 in. long, 0.5–0.625 in. wide; pendant, green to red

PLANT HEIGHT 24–30 in.

HARVEST Midseason, 70–80 days after transplanting

HEAT LEVEL Hot

Prolific. Used in fresh salsas and Mexican cuisine.

Hidalgo

Capsicum annuum 'Hidalgo'

ORIGIN Mexico

PODS 2–2.5 in. long, 0.5–0.625 in. wide; pendant, green to red

PLANT HEIGHT 18–24 in.

HARVEST Midseason, 70–80 days after transplanting

HEAT LEVEL Hot

Prolific. Used in Mexican cuisine and fresh salsas.

Huasteco

Capsicum annuum 'Huasteco'

ORIGIN Mexico

PODS 2–2.5 in. long, 0.5–0.625 in. wide; upright, green to red

PLANT HEIGHT 18–24 in.

HARVEST Midseason, 70–80 days after transplanting

HEAT LEVEL Hot

Prolific; an improved variety. Used in Mexican cuisine and fresh salsas.

Serrano

Capsicum annuum 'Serrano'

ORIGIN Mexico

PODS 2–2.5 in. long, 0.375–0.5 in. wide; pendant, green to red

PLANT HEIGHT 18–24 in.

HARVEST Midseason, 70–80 days after transplanting

HEAT LEVEL Hot

Used in Mexican cuisine and fresh salsas.

Serrano Del Sol Hybrid

Capsicum annuum 'Serrano Del Sol Hybrid'

ORIGIN Mexico

PODS 2.5–3.5 in. long, 0.5–0.75 in. wide; pendant, green to red

PLANT HEIGHT 18–24 in.

HARVEST Midseason, 70–80 days after transplanting

HEAT LEVEL Hot

A newer hybrid serrano. Prolific; disease resistant. Used in fresh salsas and Mexican cuisine.

Serrano Purple

Capsicum annuum 'Serrano Purple'

ORIGIN Unknown

PODS 2–3 in. long, 0.75–1 in. wide; pendant, green to purple to red

PLANT HEIGHT 18–24 in.

HARVEST Midseason, 70–80 days after transplanting

HEAT LEVEL Hot

Used in Mexican cuisine and fresh salsas.

Serrano Tampiqueño

Capsicum annuum **'Serrano Tampiqueño'**

ORIGIN Mexico

PODS 1.75–2.25 in. long, 0.5–0.625 in. wide; pendant, green to red

PLANT HEIGHT 18–24 in.

HARVEST Midseason, 70–80 days after transplanting

HEAT LEVEL Hot

A slightly smaller serrano. Prolific. Used in Mexican cuisine and fresh salsas.

Squash

This Caribbean pod type, also known as mushroom pepper, has very few varieties. The squash type is best known for the flattened shape of the pods, which are often mistaken for Scotch bonnets. Most plants of the squash type are multistemmed with a habit that is subcompact tending toward prostrate, growing to 18–24 inches tall. The leaves are medium green, ovate to lanceolate, and smooth. The flower corollas are white with no spots. The pods are flattened and have a squashlike shape, measuring about 1–1½ inches long and 1½ inches wide. The pods are green, turning yellow or red at maturity, and are also excellent for pickling. In Jamaica, they are used in hot sauces and jerk seasoning when Scotch bonnets are not available.

Jamaican Gold

Capsicum annuum 'Jamaican Gold'

ORIGIN Jamaica

PODS 1–1.5 in. long, 1.25–1.75 in. wide; pendant, green to golden yellow

PLANT HEIGHT 18–24 in.

HARVEST Midseason, 70–80 days after transplanting

HEAT LEVEL Hot

Prolific. Used in hot sauces and jerk seasoning. Can also be pickled.

Jamaican Red

Capsicum annuum **'Jamaican Red'**

ORIGIN Jamaica

PODS 1–1.5 in. long, 1.25–1.5 in. wide; pendant, green to red

PLANT HEIGHT 18–24 in.

HARVEST Midseason, 70–80 days after transplanting

HEAT LEVEL Hot

Prolific. Used in hot sauces and jerk seasoning. Can also be pickled.

PA 353 Red

Capsicum annuum 'PA 353 Red'

ORIGIN United States

PODS 1–1.5 in. long, 1.5–2 in. wide; pendant, green to red

PLANT HEIGHT 18–24 in.

HARVEST Midseason, 70–80 days after transplanting

HEAT LEVEL Hot

Developed by the US Vegetable Laboratory. Prolific; resistance to root-knot nematode.

Squash Red

Capsicum annuum 'Squash Red'

ORIGIN Jamaica

PODS 1.5–2 in. long and wide; pendant, green to red

PLANT HEIGHT 18–24 in.

HARVEST Midseason, 70–80 days after transplanting

HEAT LEVEL Medium

Also called 'Red Mushroom'. This prolific variety can be stuffed or pickled.

Squash Yellow

Capsicum annuum 'Squash Yellow'

ORIGIN Jamaica

PODS 1.5–2 in. long and wide; pendant, green to yellow

PLANT HEIGHT 18–24 in.

HARVEST Midseason, 70–80 days after transplanting

HEAT LEVEL Medium

Also called 'Yellow Mushroom'. This prolific variety can be stuffed or pickled.

Wax

The name of this type comes from the shiny appearance of the pods, which vary greatly in size, appearance, and pungency. 'Santa Fe Grande' has multiple stems and an erect habit, growing 18–24 inches tall. The leaves are ovate, smooth, and medium green in color. The flower corollas are white with no spots. The pods are borne pendant, conical but tapering, and bluntly pointed at the end. They begin as yellow and mature to orange and then red, and measure 3½–5 inches long and 1½ inches wide. The growing period is generally 70 or more days, and they range from 2500 to 5000 SHUs.

The pungent wax varieties were developed from the mild 'Banana Pepper', which was introduced into the United States from Hungary in 1932. One of the first pungent varieties was 'Hungarian Yellow Wax Hot', which became a popular garden and pickling chile. Another variety, which was first used exclusively as an ornamental, is 'Floral Gem', with its beautiful orange-red pods. In 1966, Paul Smith of the University of California-Davis crossed 'Floral Gem' with 'Fresno', and then crossed that hybrid with 'Hungarian Yellow Wax Hot' to produce the 'Caloro' variety, which was soon refined to become 'Santa Fe Grande'.

About 3000 acres of wax chiles are commercially cultivated in the United States, principally to produce pickled peppers. They are popular home garden varieties because of their hardiness and the beautiful colors of yellow, orange, and red fruits on the same plant.

———

Banana Hot

Capsicum annuum 'Banana Hot'

ORIGIN United States

PODS 5-7 in. long, 1-1.5 in. wide; upright to pendant, greenish yellow to red

PLANT HEIGHT 24-30 in.

HARVEST Early season, 60-70 days after transplanting

HEAT LEVEL Medium

Prolific. Used in Hungarian cuisine and for pickling.

Banana Sweet

Capsicum annuum 'Banana Sweet'

ORIGIN South America

PODS 6-7 in. long, 1.25-1.75 in. wide; pendant, greenish yellow to orange to red

PLANT HEIGHT 18-24 in.

HARVEST Early season, 60-70 days after transplanting

HEAT LEVEL Sweet

Prolific. Used for pickling or eaten fresh.

Bananarama Hybrid

Capsicum annuum 'Bananarama Hybrid'

ORIGIN United States

PODS 6–8 in. long, 1.25–1.75 in. wide; pendant, greenish yellow to orange to red

PLANT HEIGHT 24–30 in.

HARVEST Early season, 60–70 days after transplanting

HEAT LEVEL Sweet

Prolific. Used for pickles, salads, or frying.

Cascabella

Capsicum annuum 'Cascabella'

ORIGIN South America

PODS 1.75–2.5 in. long, 0.5–1 in. wide; pendant, greenish yellow to orange to red

PLANT HEIGHT 18–24 in.

HARVEST Midseason, 70–80 days after transplanting

HEAT LEVEL Medium

Prolific. Used for pickling and in salsas.

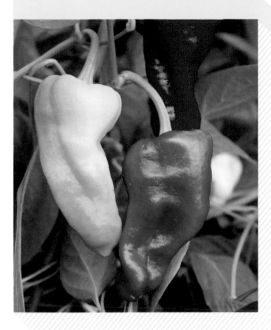

Floral Gem

Capsicum annuum 'Floral Gem'

ORIGIN United States

PODS 2–3 in. long, 0.75–1 in. wide; pendant, pale yellow to orange to red

PLANT HEIGHT 18–24 in.

HARVEST Midseason, 70–80 days after transplanting

HEAT LEVEL Medium

In terms of culinary usage, when pickled in its immature stage it is known as 'Torrido Pepper'. Good container plant.

Hinkle Hatz

Capsicum annuum 'Hinkle Hatz'

ORIGIN Netherlands and the United States (Pennsylvania)

PODS 0.75–1.25 in. long, 0.5–0.75 in. wide; pendant, green to red, sometimes green to yellow

PLANT HEIGHT 12–18 in.

HARVEST Midseason, 70–80 days after transplanting

HEAT LEVEL Very hot

An heirloom cultivated by the Pennsylvania Dutch since the 1880s. The name translates as "chicken heart" because the pods resemble a chicken's heart. Traditionally used for pickling and making pepper vinegar.

Hungarian Yellow Wax

Capsicum annuum **'Hungarian Yellow Wax'**

ORIGIN Hungary

PODS 4–6 in. long, 1–1.25 in. wide; pendant, greenish yellow to orange to red

PLANT HEIGHT 18–24 in.

HARVEST Early season, 60–70 days after transplanting

HEAT LEVEL Medium

Also known as 'Yellow Wax'. Prolific. Used for Hungarian cuisine and pickling.

Inferno Hybrid

Capsicum annuum **'Inferno Hybrid'**

ORIGIN United States

PODS 6–8 in. long, 0.75–1.25 in. long; pendant, pale yellow to red

PLANT HEIGHT 18–24 in.

HARVEST Early season, 60–70 days after transplanting

HEAT LEVEL Medium

Prolific; an improved variety with very uniform production. Used for pickling or in salsas.

Santa Fe Grande

Capsicum annuum **'Santa Fe Grande'**

ORIGIN United States (New Mexico)

PODS 3–4 in. long, 0.75–1.25 in. wide; pendant, greenish yellow to orange to red

PLANT HEIGHT 18–24 in.

HARVEST Early season, 60–70 days after transplanting

HEAT LEVEL Medium

Short wax type; prolific. Used fresh and for canning and processing.

Wenk's Yellow Hots

Capsicum annuum **'Wenk's Yellow Hots'**

ORIGIN United States (Albuquerque, New Mexico)

PODS 2–3 in. long, 0.75–1.25 in. wide; pendant, greenish yellow to orange to red

PLANT HEIGHT 18–24 in.

HARVEST Early season, 60–70 days after transplanting

HEAT LEVEL Medium

Wenk Farms, where this pepper was developed, is now a Walmart just 2 miles from coauthor Dave DeWitt's house in the south valley of Albuquerque—but at least the pepper lives on!

Capsicum baccatum

The word *baccatum* means berrylike. *Capsicum baccatum*, familiarly termed *ají* throughout South America, originated either in Bolivia or in Peru and, according to archaeological evidence, was probably domesticated in Peru about 2500 BC.

Extensive *C. baccatum* material found at the Huaca Prieta archaeological site in Peru shows that the species was gradually improved by the pre-Incan civilizations.

Fruit size increased and the fruits gradually became nondeciduous and stayed on the plants through ripening. There are at least two wild forms (*baccatum* and *microcarpum*) and many domesticated forms. The domesticated ajís have a great diversity of pod shape and size, ranging from short, pointed pods borne erect to long, pendant pods resembling the New Mexican varieties. One variety of ají, puca-uchu, grows on a vinelike plant in home gardens. The species is generally distinguished from others by the yellow or tan spots on the corollas of the flowers, and by the yellow anthers.

Capsicum baccatum is cultivated in Argentina, Colombia, Ecuador, Peru, Brazil, and Bolivia, and the species has been introduced into Costa Rica, India, and the United States. In the United States, it is grown to a very limited extent in California under the brand name Mild Italian and in Nevada under the brand name Chileno.

Ajís are tall, sometimes reaching 5 feet, and have multiple stems and an erect habit, occasionally tending toward sprawling. The large leaves are dark green, measuring up to 7 inches long and 4 inches wide. The pods usually begin erect and become pendant; as they mature, they are elongate in shape, measure between 3–6 inches long and ¾–1½ inches wide. They usually mature to an orange-red, but yellow and brown colors also appear in some varieties. The pods typically measure between 30,000 and 50,000 SHUs.

Capsicum baccatum plants tend to stand out in the garden like small trees. Their growing period is up to 120 days or more after transplanting, and the plants can produce 40 or more pods. The pods have a distinctive, fruity flavor and are used fresh in ceviche (lime-marinated fish) in South America. They are also used fresh in salsas and the small yellow varieties are prized for their lemony aroma. The pods of all ajís can also be dried in the sun and then crushed into colorful powders.

———

Ají Benito

Capsicum baccatum 'Ají Benito'

ORIGIN Bolivia

PODS 2.5–3 in. long, 0.75–1 in. wide; pendant, green to orange to red

PLANT HEIGHT 24–30 in.

HARVEST Late season, 80–90 days after transplanting

HEAT LEVEL Hot

Prolific. A very tasty ají; used dried in sauces.

Ají Cito

Capsicum baccatum 'Ají Cito'

ORIGIN Peru

PODS 2.5–3.5 in. long, 0.75–1 in. wide; pendant, green to gold

PLANT HEIGHT 24–30 in.

HARVEST Late season, 80–90 days after transplanting

HEAT LEVEL Hot

Prolific. Among the hottest of the species; used for hot sauce.

Ají Colorado

Capsicum baccatum 'Ají Colorado'

ORIGIN Bolivia and Peru

PODS 3–5 in. long, 0.75–1 in. wide; pendant, green to red

PLANT HEIGHT 30–36 in.

HARVEST Very late season, 90 or more days after transplanting

HEAT LEVEL Hot

Prolific, with slightly wrinkled, shiny pods. Used for hot sauce and chile paste.

Ají Cristal

Capsicum baccatum 'Ají Cristal'

ORIGIN Chile

PODS 3–3.5 in. long, 0.75–1.25 in. wide; pendant, greenish yellow to orange to red.

PLANT HEIGHT 24–30 in.

HARVEST Midseason, 70–80 days after transplanting

HEAT LEVEL Medium

Flavor is best when pods are immature. Used for hot sauce.

Ají Habanero

Capsicum baccatum **'Ají Habanero'**

ORIGIN South America

PODS 2–2.5 in. long, 0.5–0.75 in. wide; pendant, pale yellow to orange

PLANT HEIGHT 18–24 in.

HARVEST Midseason, 70–80 days after transplanting

HEAT LEVEL Mild

As yet another example of confusing nomenclature, this pepper is not from Havana, doesn't look like the *C. chinense* habaneros, and is mild—so why is it called habanero? We have no idea. Used as a seasoning pepper.

Ají Omnicolor

Capsicum baccatum **'Ají Omnicolor'**

ORIGIN Peru

PODS 2–2.5 in. long, 0.5–0.625 in. wide; pendant, pale yellow to purple splotched to yellow to orange to red

PLANT HEIGHT 18–24 in.

HARVEST Midseason, 70–80 days after transplanting

HEAT LEVEL Hot

A real beauty in the garden with excellent flavor. Can be used for ornamental purposes.

Ají Rojo

Capsicum baccatum 'Ají Rojo'

ORIGIN Peru

PODS 4–6 in. long, 0.75–1 in. wide; pendant, green to deep orange

PLANT HEIGHT 30-36 in.

HARVEST Very late season, 90 or more days after transplanting

HEAT LEVEL Hot

Also known as 'Ají Amarillo'. Prolific; coauthor Dave's plants grew to 5 feet tall in Albuquerque, NM. Used for hot sauces and chile powder.

Amarillear

Capsicum baccatum 'Amarillear'

ORIGIN South America

PODS 0.375–0.5 in. long, 0.25–0.375 in. wide; upright, green to orange to red

PLANT HEIGHT 30–36 in.

HARVEST Midseason, 70–80 days after transplanting

HEAT LEVEL Hot

A very small *C. baccatum*. Used for hot sauce and chile powder.

Bishops Crown

Capsicum baccatum **'Bishops Crown'**

ORIGIN Barbados

PODS 1–1.5 in. long, 2–2.5 in. wide; pendant, light green to orange to red

PLANT HEIGHT 30–36 in.

HARVEST Very late season, 90 or more days after transplanting

HEAT LEVEL Medium

Unusually shaped fruit that flanges out, also known as 'Christmas Bell', 'Peri-Peri', or 'Joker's Hat'.

Brazilian Starfish

Capsicum baccatum 'Brazilian Starfish'

ORIGIN Brazil

PODS 0.75–1 in. long, 1.25–1.5 in. wide; pendant, green to bright red

PLANT HEIGHT 30–36 in.

HARVEST Late season, 80–90 days after transplanting

HEAT LEVEL Hot

Also known as 'Starfish'. Unusual fruits are flattened, with scalloped edges.

C. Baccatum Gold

Capsicum baccatum 'C. Baccatum Gold'

ORIGIN South America

PODS 2–3 in. long, 0.375–0.5 in. wide; pendant, green to golden yellow

PLANT HEIGHT 24–30 in.

HARVEST Midseason, 70–80 days after transplanting

HEAT LEVEL Medium

Prolific. Used for hot sauce and chile powder.

Christmas Bell

Capsicum baccatum **'Christmas Bell'**

ORIGIN South America

PODS 2–2.5 in. long and wide; pendant, pale green to orange to red

PLANT HEIGHT 30–36 in.

HARVEST Very late season, 90 or more days after transplanting

HEAT LEVEL Mild

Also known as 'Orchid', 'Ají Flor', and 'Tulip'. Unusually shaped fruit. Used as seasoning pepper. Similar to 'Bishop's Crown', though the fruits of this variety don't flange as much.

Dedo de Moca

Capsicum baccatum **'Dedo de Moca'**

ORIGIN South America

PODS 2.5–3 in. long, 0.5–0.75 in. wide; pendant, green to bright red

PLANT HEIGHT 24–30 in. tall

HARVEST Late season, 80–90 days after transplanting

HEAT LEVEL Medium

Used for sauces, chile powder, and chutneys.

Inca Red Drop

Capsicum baccatum **'Inca Red Drop'**

ORIGIN Peru

PODS 1–1.5 in. long, 0.5–0.75 in. wide; upright, yellowish green to orange to bright red

PLANT HEIGHT 18–24 in.

HARVEST Midseason, 70–80 days after transplanting

HEAT LEVEL Hot

Used for chile powder and fresh salsas.

Lemon Drop

Capsicum baccatum **'Lemon Drop'**

ORIGIN Peru

PODS 2–3 in. long, 0.5–0.75 in. wide; pendant, green to bright yellow

PLANT HEIGHT 24–30 in.

HARVEST Late season, 80–90 days after transplanting

HEAT LEVEL Hot

Lemony aroma. Used for chile powder and fresh salsas.

Peanut

Capsicum baccatum 'Peanut'

ORIGIN South America

PODS 2–3 in. long, 0.75–1 in. wide; upright to pendant, green to orange to red

PLANT HEIGHT 24–30 in.

HARVEST Late season, 80–90 days after transplanting

HEAT LEVEL Hot

Used dried in chile powder, and fresh is salsas and sauces.

Peru Yellow

Capsicum baccatum 'Peru Yellow'

ORIGIN Peru

PODS 2–3 in. long, 0.5–0.75 in. wide; pendant, green to bright yellow

PLANT HEIGHT 24–30 in.

HARVEST Late season, 80–90 days after transplanting

HEAT LEVEL Hot

Used for chile powder and fresh salsas.

Pilange

Capsicum baccatum **'Pilange'**

ORIGIN Peru

PODS 0.5–0.75 in. long, 1–1.25 in. wide; pendant, dark green to orange to red

PLANT HEIGHT 24–30 in.

HARVEST Late season, 80–90 days after transplanting

HEAT LEVEL Medium

Used for chile powder and fresh salsas.

White Wax

Capsicum baccatum **'White Wax'**

ORIGIN Unknown

PODS 3–4 in. long, 0.5–1 in. wide; pendant, pale yellow to orange to red

PLANT HEIGHT 24–30 in.

HARVEST Late season, 80–90 days after transplanting

HEAT LEVEL Medium

The pods are usually pickled in the immature (yellow) phase.

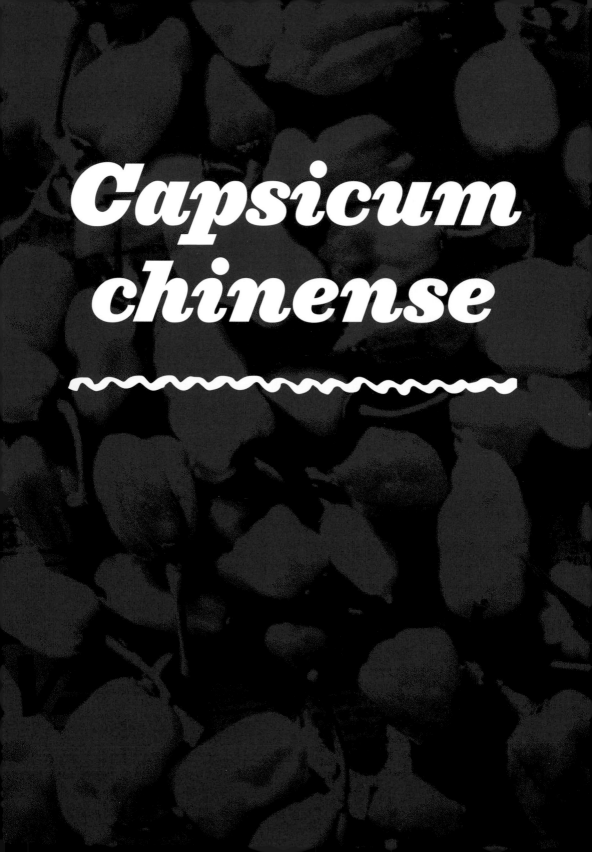

Capsicum chinense

This entire species is often referred to as "habaneros," but that appellation is a misnomer because there are hundreds of varieties, and the name habanero refers to a specific pod type from the Yucatán Peninsula of Mexico.

The Amazon basin was the center of origin for *C. chinense*, a species famous for having the hottest peppers of them all. The oldest known *C. chinense* plant ever found was the still-intact 6500-year-old pod in Guitarrero Cave in Peru.

Bernabé Cobo, a naturalist who traveled throughout South America during the early seventeenth century, was probably the first European to study the species. He estimated that there were at least forty different varieties, "some as large as limes or large plums; others, as small as pine nuts or even grains of wheat, and between the two extremes are many different sizes. No less variety is found in color . . . and the same difference is found in form and shape."

The species was first noted in 1768 in Philip Miller's *A Gardener's Dictionary*, where it was identified as *C. angulofum*, a West Indian pepper with wrinkled leaves and a bonnet shape. The species was then (mis)named *C. chinense* in 1776 by Nikolaus von Jacquin, a Dutch physician who collected plants in the Caribbean for Emperor Francis I from 1754–1759. Jacquin, who first used this name in his *Hortus botanicus vindobonensis*, wrote, mysteriously, "I have taken the plant's name from its homeland." Why would Jacquin write that a plant native to the West Indies was from China? Jacquin had never collected plants in China, and considering the fact that the first Chinese laborers to the West Indies would not arrive in Cuba until the early 1800s, it is unlikely that Jacquin crossed paths with any suspected Chinese "importers" of the species. It is likely that this pepper mystery will never be solved, so we are stuck with a totally inaccurate species name of a supposedly Chinese pepper that's not from China. And, so far, no taxonomist has gone out on a limb to correct this obvious error.

With a great diversity of pod shapes and heat levels ranging from zero to well over a million SHUs, *Capsicum chinense* is the most important cultivated pepper east of the Andes in South America. The seeds were carried and cultivated by Native Americans and the species hopped, skipped, and jumped around the

West Indies, forming—seemingly on each island—specifically adapted pod types that are called land races of the species. These land races were given local names in the various islands and countries, although the names Scotch bonnet, goat pepper, and habanero are also used generically throughout the region.

In the eastern Caribbean, habanero relatives are called Congo peppers in Trinidad and booney or bonney peppers in Barbados. In the French Caribbean islands of Martinique and Guadeloupe, the hot peppers are known as "le derriere de Madame Jacques," and in Haiti, they are called *piment bouc*, or goat pepper. In the western Caribbean, you'll find the familiar Jamaican Scotch bonnets, Puerto Rican rocotillos, and the Cuban *cachucha* ("cap") peppers. These land races and their colorful names became the dominant spicy element in the food of the Caribbean.

Capsicum chinense varieties range from 1–4½ feet tall, depending on variety and environmental factors. Some varieties grown as perennials have reached 8 feet tall in tropical climates, but the average height in US gardens is approximately 24 inches. Plants have multiple stems and a compact habit. The leaves are pale to medium green, large, and wrinkled. The flowers have off-white corollas and purple anthers. The plant sets two to six fruits per node.

The pods of *C. chinense* vary enormously in size and shape, ranging from chiltepín-sized berries a quarter-inch in diameter to wrinkled and elongated pods up to 5 inches long. The familiar habaneros are pendant, campanulate (shaped like a flattened bell), and some are pointed at the end. Caribbean *C. chinense* are often flattened at the end and resemble a tam, or bonnet. The blossom ends of these pods are frequently inverted. The pods are green at immaturity and usually mature to red, orange, yellow, purple, and brown. *Capsicum chinense* pods are characterized by a distinctive, fruity aroma that is often described as "apricotlike." Interestingly enough, that aroma is present regardless of the variety, heat level, or the size of the pod.

The heat level of the species has been the subject of much discussion. Phrases like "hottest pepper in the world" and "a thousand times hotter a jalapeño" have been bandied about for years, but they don't really tell the story. In actuality, the species does have nonpungent varieties, just like the bell peppers of *C. annuum*. Although *C. chinense* varieties range in heat from zero to the hottest ever measured, they average between 80,000 and 150,000 SHUs, with the hottest pod ever recorded, 'Smokin' Ed's Carolina Reaper', at 1.569 million SHUs. In terms of the average number of SHUs, a habanero, for example, is about 50 times hotter than a jalapeño—as measured by a chromatograph, not the human mouth. Because humans have varying numbers of capsaicin receptors, reactions can vary enormously from person to person.

Another member of the species that is commonly used, especially in the eastern Caribbean, is the seasoning pepper. It is a mild to medium hot, elongated pepper that is used in quantity for seasoning pastes in Trinidad, Barbados, St. Lucia, and other islands.

In the Yucatán Peninsula the species is called habanero, which means "from Havana," hinting of a transference to Mexico from the Caribbean. It has long been rumored that habaneros no longer grow in Cuba, but pepper aficionado Richard Rice sent us seeds in 1990 given to him by Cuban refugees. The seeds did indeed produce habaneros, which would suggest that they are still grown in Cuba today. The species was transferred to Africa during the colonization of Brazil or during the later traffic in slaves, and today there are many *C. chinense* varieties in Africa.

The seeds tend to take a long time to germinate. Being tropical plants, they do best in areas with high humidity and warm nights. They are slow growers, especially in the hot, dry Southwest, and the growing period is 80–120 days or more after transplanting. The yield varies enormously according to how well the particular plants adapt to the local environment.

Habaneros are grown commercially in the Yucatán Peninsula of Mexico, where about 1500 tons a year are harvested. They are cultivated to a lesser extent in Belize and there are small commercial fields of other *C. chinense* varieties in Jamaica, Trinidad, and to a limited extent on other islands, such as the Bahamas. In the United States, there are several commercial growing operations from South Carolina west to California. The datil pepper, a milder *C. chinense* variety grown for about 300 years in St. Augustine, Florida, is processed into sauces and jellies.

The *C. chinense* pods are used fresh in salsas and are commonly used to make extremely hot, liquid sauces when combined with carrots and onions. They can be dried and ground into powder, but be sure to wear a protective mask when doing so.

7 Pot

Capsicum chinense '7 Pot'

ORIGIN Trinidad

PODS 1.75–2 in. long, 1.25–1.375 in. wide; pendant, green to red

PLANT HEIGHT 24–30 in.

HARVEST Extremely late season, 120 or more days after transplanting

HEAT LEVEL Super hot

Gnarly and pimply pods, one pod for "7 pots" of stew. Used to make extremely hot sauces. This is the Jonah strain.

7 Pot Douglah

Capsicum chinense '7 Pot Douglah'

ORIGIN Trinidad

PODS 2–2.25 in. long, 1–1.25 in. wide; pendant, green to brown

PLANT HEIGHT 24–30 in.

HARVEST Extremely late season, 120 or more days after transplanting

HEAT LEVEL Super hot

A chocolate version of '7 Pot'. Used to make extremely hot sauces.

7 Pot Yellow

Capsicum chinense '7 Pot Yellow'

ORIGIN Trinidad

PODS 1.5–2 in. long, 1.25–1.375 in. wide; pendant, green to yellow

PLANT HEIGHT 24–30 in.

HARVEST Extremely late season, 120 or more days after transplanting

HEAT LEVEL Extremely hot

This is the yellow version of '7 Pot'. Used to make extremely hot sauces.

Ají Brown

Capsicum chinense 'Ají Brown'

ORIGIN South America

PODS 4–6 in. long, 0.5–1 in. wide; pendant, green to deep brown

PLANT HEIGHT 24–30 in.

HARVEST Very late season, 90 or more days after transplanting

HEAT LEVEL Mild

Sweet, rich flavor with very little heat. Used dried. Note that *ají* is a generic term for all kinds of chiles in South America.

Ají Dulce 1

Capsicum chinense 'Ají Dulce 1'

ORIGIN South America

PODS 1–2 in. long, 1–1.25 in. wide; pendant, pale green to orange to red

PLANT HEIGHT 24–30 in.

HARVEST Late season, 80–90 days after transplanting

HEAT LEVEL Mild

Flavor and aroma of a habanero, but without the heat. Used as a seasoning pepper.

Ají Dulce 2

Capsicum chinense 'Ají Dulce 2'

ORIGIN Venezuela

PODS 1–2 in. long, 1–1.25 in. wide; pendant, green to orange to red

PLANT HEIGHT 18 24 in.

HARVEST Late season, 80–90 days after transplanting

HEAT LEVEL Mild

Flavor, aroma, and shape of a habanero, but without the heat. Used as a seasoning pepper.

Ají Panca

Capsicum chinense 'Ají Panca'

ORIGIN Peru

PODS 4–6 in. long, 0.5–1 in. wide; pendant, green to deep brown

PLANT HEIGHT 24–30 in.

HARVEST Very late season, 90 or more days after transplanting

HEAT LEVEL Mild

Fruits have rich sweet flavor with little heat. Used dried.

Capsicum chinense

Ají Yellow 2

Capsicum chinense 'Ají Yellow 2'

ORIGIN Peru

PODS 2.5–3.5 in. long, 0.5–0.75 in. wide; pedant, green to bright yellow

PLANT HEIGHT 18–24 in.

HARVEST Late season, 80–90 days after transplanting

HEAT LEVEL Hot

Prolific. Used fresh, as well as for chile powder and hot sauce.

Amazon

Capsicum chinense 'Amazon'

ORIGIN Unknown

PODS 2–2.5 in. long, 0.75–1.25 in. wide; pendant, green to bright yellow

PLANT HEIGHT 24–30 in.

HARVEST Late season, 80–90 days after transplanting

HEAT LEVEL Very hot

Prolific. Used for chile powder, hot sauce, and jerk and rub seasoning.

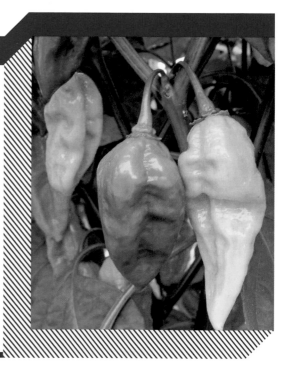

Antillais Caribbean

Capsicum chinense 'Antillais Caribbean'

ORIGIN Caribbean Basin

PODS 2–2.5 in. long, 1.5–2 in. wide; pendant, light green to orange to red

PLANT HEIGHT 24–30 in.

HARVEST Late season, 80–90 days after transplanting

HEAT LEVEL Very hot

Used for chile powder and hot sauce.

Aribibi Gusano

Capsicum chinense 'Aribibi Gusano'

ORIGIN Bolivia

PODS 1–1.5 in. long, 0.25–0.5 in. wide; pendant, green to pale yellow to creamy white

PLANT HEIGHT 12–18 in.

HARVEST Late season, 80–90 days after transplanting

HEAT LEVEL Very hot

Prolific; unusual, worm-shaped fruit. Sometimes known as 'Caterpillar Pepper'.

Australian Lantern Red

Capsicum chinense **'Australian Lantern Red'**

ORIGIN Australia

PODS 0.75–1 in. long, 0.5–0.625 in. wide; pendant, green to orange to red

PLANT HEIGHT 24–30 in.

HARVEST Very late season, 90 or more days after transplanting

HEAT LEVEL Very hot

Prolific; diamond-shaped fruit. Used for chile powder and hot sauce.

Barbados

Capsicum chinense **'Barbados'**

ORIGIN Barbados

PODS 1.5–2 in. long, 1.25–1.75 in. wide; pendant, green to red

PLANT HEIGHT 24–30 in.

HARVEST Late season, 80–90 days after transplanting

HEAT LEVEL Very hot

Also known as 'Bonney Pepper'. Used for chile powder and hot sauce.

Bazuka

Capsicum chinense 'Bazuka'

ORIGIN Guadeloupe

PODS 1.5–2 in. long, 1.25–1.5 in. wide; pendant, pale green to orange to red

PLANT HEIGHT 24–30 in.

HARVEST Late season, 80–90 days after transplanting

HEAT LEVEL Very hot

Used for chile powder and hot sauce.

Beni Highlands

Capsicum chinense 'Beni Highlands'

ORIGIN Bolivia

PODS 1.5–2 in. long, 0.5–0.625 in. wide; pendant, green to golden yellow

PLANT HEIGHT 12–18 in.

HARVEST Early season, 60–70 days after transplanting

HEAT LEVEL Hot

An early-maturing habanero type, good for cool-season climates; prolific. Used for chile powder and hot sauce.

Bhut Jolokia

Capsicum chinense 'Bhut Jolokia'

ORIGIN India by way of Trinidad

PODS 2–3 in. long, 1–1.5 in. wide; pendant, green to orange to red

PLANT HEIGHT 24–30 in.

HARVEST Extremely late season, 120 or more days after transplanting

HEAT LEVEL Super hot

Frequently known as 'Ghost Pepper', the chile that started the super-hot craze. It was previously listed by *Guinness World Records* from 2007–2011 as the hottest known chile, with a rating of 1 million SHUs! Used for chile powder and hot sauce.

Bhut Jolokia Assam

Capsicum chinense 'Bhut Jolokia Assam'

ORIGIN India (Assam)

PODS 2–3 in. long, 1–1.75 in. wide; pendant, green to red

PLANT HEIGHT 24–30 in.

HARVEST Extremely late season, 120 or more days after transplanting

HEAT LEVEL Super hot

This strain is a bit fuller and plumper than the usual 'Bhut Jolokia'. Used for chile powder and hot sauce.

Bhut Jolokia Peach

Capsicum chinense 'Bhut Jolokia Peach'

ORIGIN United States

PODS 2.5–3.5 in. long, 0.75–1.25 in. wide; pendant, pale green to peach

PLANT HEIGHT 24–30 in.

HARVEST Extremely late season, 120 or more days after transplanting

HEAT LEVEL Extremely hot

This is the peach version of 'Bhut Jolokia'. Used for chile powder and hot sauce.

Bhut Jolokia White

Capsicum chinense 'Bhut Jolokia White'

ORIGIN United States

PODS 2–3 in. long, 0.75–1.25 in. wide; pendant, pale green to creamy white

PLANT HEIGHT 24–30 in.

HARVEST Late season, 80–90 days after transplanting

HEAT LEVEL Extremely hot

Another elongated variety of 'Bhut Jolokia' with an unusual white pod color.

Bhut Jolokia Yellow

Capsicum chinense 'Bhut Jolokia Yellow'

ORIGIN India

PODS 2.5–3.5 in. long, 1–1.25 in. wide; pendant, green to yellow

PLANT HEIGHT 24–30 in.

HARVEST Extremely late season, 120 or more days after transplanting

HEAT LEVEL Extremely hot

Another color of the famous 'Ghost Pepper'. Used for chile powder and hot sauce.

Billy Goat

Capsicum chinense 'Billy Goat'

ORIGIN Bahamas

PODS 0.5–0.75 in. long and wide; pendant, green to orange to dark red

PLANT HEIGHT 24–30 in.

HARVEST Very late season, 90 or more days after transplanting

HEAT LEVEL Very hot

Prolific. Fruit has a hint of cherry aroma. Used for chile powder and hot sauce.

Black Cayman

Capsicum chinense 'Black Cayman'

ORIGIN Cayman Islands

PODS 1.5–2.5 in. long, 1.25–1.75 in. wide; pendant, green to dark brown

PLANT HEIGHT 24–30 in.

HARVEST Late season, 80–90 days after transplanting

HEAT LEVEL Very hot

Used for chile powder and hot sauce.

Bod'e

Capsicum chinense 'Bod'e'

ORIGIN Brazil

PODS 0.375–0.5 in. long and wide; upright, pale green to orange to red

PLANT HEIGHT 24–30 in.

HARVEST Late season, 80–90 days after transplanting

HEAT LEVEL Very hot

Also known as 'Bode'. Prolific. Fruit has a hint of cherry flavor. Used for ornamental purposes and for hot sauce.

Bonda Ma Jacques

Capsicum chinense 'Bonda Ma Jacques'

ORIGIN Guadalupe

PODS 2–2.25 in. long, 1–1.25 in. wide; pendant, green to yellow

PLANT HEIGHT 24–30 in.

HARVEST Late season, 80–90 days after transplanting

HEAT LEVEL Very hot

Used for chile powder, hot sauce, and jerk seasoning.

Burkina Yellow

Capsicum chinense 'Burkina Yellow'

ORIGIN Burkina Faso, Africa

PODS 1.5–2 in. long, 1–1.25 in. wide; pendant, pale green to yellow

PLANT HEIGHT 18–24 in.

HARVEST Late season, 80–90 days after transplanting

HEAT LEVEL Very hot

Used for chile powder, hot sauce, and jerk seasoning.

Caiene

Capsicum chinense 'Caiene'

ORIGIN Brazil

PODS 1.5–2.25 in. long, 1–1.25 in. wide; pendant, green to orange to red

PLANT HEIGHT 24–30 in.

HARVEST Late season, 80–90 days after transplanting

HEAT LEVEL Very hot

Used for chile powder and hot sauce.

Caribbean Red

Capsicum chinense 'Caribbean Red'

ORIGIN Caribbean Basin

PODS 1.5–1.75 in. long, 1–1.5 in. wide; pendant, green to orange to red

PLANT HEIGHT 24–30 in.

HARVEST Late season, 80–90 days after transplanting

HEAT LEVEL Very hot

Prolific. Used for chile powder and hot sauce.

Carmine

Capsicum chinense 'Carmine'

ORIGIN Unknown

PODS 2–3 in. long, 1–1.25 in. wide; pendant, green to golden yellow

PLANT HEIGHT 18–24 in.

HARVEST Midseason, 70–80 days after transplanting

HEAT LEVEL Very hot

Used for chile powder and hot sauce

Cheiro

Capsicum chinense 'Cheiro'

ORIGIN Brazil

PODS 0.5–0.625 long and wide; pendant, green to purple splotched to golden orange

PLANT HEIGHT 24–30 in.

HARVEST Late season, 80–90 days after transplanting

HEAT LEVEL Very hot

Closely related to 'Bod'e'.

Chupetinho

Capsicum chinense **'Chupetinho'**

ORIGIN Brazil

PODS 0.75–1.25 in. long, 0.5–0.75 in. wide; pendant, pale green to orange to red

PLANT HEIGHT 18–24 in.

HARVEST Late season, 80–90 days after transplanting

HEAT LEVEL Medium

Prolific. Nipple-shaped fruits used for chile powder, hot sauce, and as seasoning pepper.

Cleo's Dragon

Capsicum chinense 'Cleo's Dragon'

ORIGIN Unknown

PODS 2.5–3 in. long, and wide; pendant, pale green to orange to red

PLANT HEIGHT 24–30 in.

HARVEST Late season, 80–90 days after transplanting

HEAT LEVEL Very hot

A larger habanero. Used for chile powder and hot sauce.

Condor's Beak

Capsicum chinense 'Condor's Beak'

ORIGIN South America

PODS 1.5–2 in. long, 0.5–0.75 in. wide; pendant, creamy green to purple to red

PLANT HEIGHT 24–30 in.

HARVEST Late season, 80–90 days after transplanting

HEAT LEVEL Very hot

An elongated habanero type. Used for pickling, chile powder, and hot sauces.

Congo Trinidad

Capsicum chinense 'Congo Trinidad'

ORIGIN Trinidad

PODS 1.5–2 in. long, 1.5–2 in. wide; pendant, green to orange to red

PLANT HEIGHT 24–30 in.

HARVEST Late season, 80–90 days after transplanting

HEAT LEVEL Very hot

A larger habanero. Used for chile powder and hot sauce.

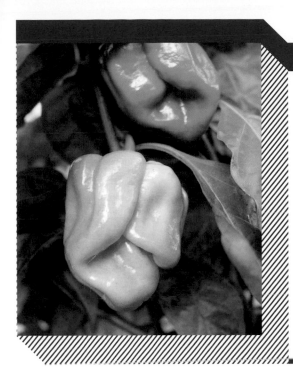

Congo Yellow Trinidad

Capsicum chinense 'Congo Yellow Trinidad'

ORIGIN Trinidad

PODS 2.5–3 in. long, 1.25–1.75 in. wide; pendant, green to golden yellow

PLANT HEIGHT 24–30 in.

HARVEST Late season, 80–90 days after transplanting

HEAT LEVEL Very hot

Large, fleshy pods. Used for chile powder and hot sauce.

Datil

Capsicum chinense 'Datil'

ORIGIN United States (St. Augustine, Florida)

PODS 2–2.5 in. long, 0.75–1 in. wide; pendant, green to golden orange

PLANT HEIGHT 24–30 in.

HARVEST Very late season, 90 or more days after transplanting

HEAT LEVEL Hot

A famous St. Augustine land race with a smoky flavor. Used for chile powder, pickling, and hot sauce.

Datil Sweet

Capsicum chinense 'Datil Sweet'

ORIGIN United States (St. Augustine, Florida)

PODS 1.5–2 in. long, 0.75–1 in. wide; pendant, pale green to orange to red

PLANT HEIGHT 24–30 in.

HARVEST Late season, 80–90 days after transplanting

HEAT LEVEL Sweet

Prolific. This pepper shares the smoky flavor of 'Datil' without the heat. Used as a seasoning pepper.

Devil's Tongue

Capsicum chinense 'Devil's Tongue'

ORIGIN United States (Pennsylvania)

PODS 2–3 in. long, 1–1.5 in. wide; pendant, green to golden yellow

PLANT HEIGHT 24–30 in.

HARVEST Very late season, 90 or more days after transplanting

HEAT LEVEL Extremely hot

An outrageously hot pepper used for chile powder, hot sauce, and jerk and rub seasoning.

Fatalii

Capsicum chinense 'Fatalii'

ORIGIN Central African Republic

PODS 2.5–3.5 in. long, 1.25–1.5 in. wide; pendant, green to bright yellow

PLANT HEIGHT 24–30 in.

HARVEST Very late season, 90 or more days after transplanting

HEAT LEVEL Extremely hot

Prolific. A deadly hot pepper used for chile powder, hot sauce, and jerk and rub seasoning.

Fatalii Red

Capsicum chinense 'Fatalii Red'

ORIGIN United States

PODS 3–4 in. long, 1–1.5 in. wide; pendant, green to red

PLANT HEIGHT 24–30 in.

HARVEST Very late season, 90 or more days after transplanting

HEAT LEVEL Extremely hot

The red version of the notorious 'Fatalii'. Used for chile powder and hot sauce.

Goat Pepper

Capsicum chinense 'Goat Pepper'

ORIGIN Bahamas

PODS 0.5–1 in. long and wide; pendant, pale green to orange to red

PLANT HEIGHT 24–30 in.

HARVEST Late season, 80–90 days after transplanting

HEAT LEVEL Very hot

A smaller-fruiting habanero type. Used for chile powder and hot sauce.

Grenada Hot

Capsicum chinense 'Grenada Hot'

ORIGIN Grenada

PODS 1.75–2 in. long, 1.25–1.5 in. wide; pendant, pale green to orange to red

PLANT HEIGHT 24–30 in.

HARVEST Late season, 80–90 days after transplanting

HEAT LEVEL Very hot

Collected from a small store during coauthor Janie's trip to the south Caribbean. Used for chile powder and hot sauce.

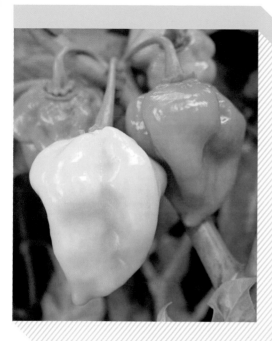

Grenada Seasoning

Capsicum chinense 'Grenada Seasoning'

ORIGIN Grenada

PODS 1.75–2 in. long, 1.25–1.5 in. wide; pendant, green to bright yellow

PLANT HEIGHT 30–36 in.

HARVEST Extremely late, 120 or more days after transplanting

HEAT LEVEL Mild

This pepper has very little heat, but is full of flavor and aroma. Used as a seasoning pepper.

Capiscum chinense

Habanero Black

Capsicum chinense 'Habanero Black'

ORIGIN Unknown

PODS 3–4 in. long, 1–1.25 in. wide; pendant, green to brown

PLANT HEIGHT 24–30 in.

HARVEST Late season, 80–90 days after transplanting

HEAT LEVEL Very hot

Used for chile powder and hot sauce.

Habanero Chocolate

Capsicum chinense 'Habanero Chocolate'

ORIGIN United States

PODS 1.5–2.5 in. long, 1–1.2 in. wide; pendant, green to chocolate brown

PLANT HEIGHT 24–30 in.

HARVEST Very late season, 90 or more days after transplanting

HEAT LEVEL Extremely hot

Also known as 'Congo Black'. Used for chile powder and hot sauce.

Habanero Francisca

Capsicum chinense 'Habanero Francisca'

ORIGIN United States (California)

PODS 2–3 in. long, 1–1.5 in. wide; pendant, green to orange

PLANT HEIGHT 24–30 in.

HARVEST Late season, 80–90 days after transplanting

HEAT LEVEL Very hot

This is a protected plant variety developed by Frank Garcia of GNS Spices, and named after Frank's grandmother. Cross Country Nurseries is a licensed grower. Related to 'Habanero Red Savina'.

Habanero Golden

Capsicum chinense **'Habanero Golden'**

ORIGIN United States

PODS 2-3 in. long, 1.5-2 in. wide; pendant, green to golden yellow

PLANT HEIGHT 24-30 in.

HARVEST Late season, 80-90 days after transplanting

HEAT LEVEL Very hot

Used for chile powder, hot sauce, and jerk and rub seasoning.

Habanero Long Chocolate

Capsicum chinense **'Habanero Long Chocolate'**

ORIGIN United States

PODS 3-4 in. long, 0.75-1.25 in. wide; pendant, green to dark brown

PLANT HEIGHT 24-30 in.

HARVEST Late season, 80-90 days after transplanting

HEAT LEVEL Hot

A bit milder than 'Habanero Chocolate' with longer pods. Used for chile powder and hot sauce. Cross Country Nurseries introduced this variety when this longer pod grew out from 'Habanero Chocolate' plants.

Habanero Mustard

Capsicum chinense 'Habanero Mustard'

ORIGIN United States

PODS 2–2.5 in. long, 1.5–1.75 in. wide; pendant, pale green to brownish orange

PLANT HEIGHT 24–30 in.

HARVEST Very late season, 90 or more days after transplanting

HEAT LEVEL Very hot

A different color among habaneros. Used for chile powder and hot sauce.

Habanero Orange

Capsicum chinense 'Habanero Orange'

ORIGIN Mexico (Yucatán Peninsula)

PODS 1.5–2.5 in. long, 1–1.5 in. wide; pendant, green to bright orange

PLANT HEIGHT 24–30 in.

HARVEST Late season, 80–90 days after transplanting

HEAT LEVEL Very hot

The most common habanero found in supermarkets. Used for chile powder and hot sauce.

Habanero Peach

Capsicum chinense 'Habanero Peach'

ORIGIN United States

PODS 1.75–2.75 in. long, 1.25–1.75 in. wide; pendant, pale green to pale yellow to pale orange

PLANT HEIGHT 24–30 in.

HARVEST Very late season, 90 or more days after transplanting

HEAT LEVEL Very hot

Used for chile powder and hot sauce.

Habanero Red

Capsicum chinense 'Habanero Red'

ORIGIN United States

PODS 1.5–2.5 in. long, 1–1.5 in. wide; pendant, green to red

PLANT HEIGHT 24–30 in.

HARVEST Late season, 80–90 days after transplanting

HEAT LEVEL Very hot

Used for chile powder and hot sauce.

Habanero Red Dominica

Capsicum chinense 'Habanero Red Dominica'

ORIGIN Dominica

PODS 1.5–2.5 in. long, 1–1.5 in. wide; pendant, green to red

PLANT HEIGHT 18–24 in.

HARVEST Late season, 80–90 days after transplanting

HEAT LEVEL Very hot

Prolific. Fleshy pods used for chile powder and hot sauce.

Habanero Red Savina

Capsicum chinense 'Habanero Red Savina'

ORIGIN United States (California)

PODS 1.5–2.5 in. long, 1–1.5 in. wide; pendant, green to red

PLANT HEIGHT 24–30 in.

HARVEST Very late season, 90 or more days after transplanting

HEAT LEVEL Extremely hot

Like 'Habanero Francisca', this was developed by Frank Garcia of GNS Spices, this time named after Frank's mother. Listed in *Guinness World Records* as the hottest pepper from 1995–2006. Cross Country Nurseries is a licensed grower.

Habanero White

Capsicum chinense 'Habanero White'

ORIGIN Yucatán Peninsula, Mexico

PODS 1.25–1.5 in. long, 0.75–1 in. wide; pendant, pale green to creamy white

PLANT HEIGHT 24–30 in.

HARVEST Late season, 80–90 days after transplanting

HEAT LEVEL Hot

Used for chile powder and hot sauce.

Habanero White 2

Capsicum chinense 'Habanero White 2'

ORIGIN Unknown

PODS 0.75–1.5 in. long, 0.375–0.5 in. wide; pendant, green to white

PLANT HEIGHT 18–24 in.

HARVEST Late season, 80–90 days after transplanting

HEAT LEVEL Very hot

Used for chile powder and hot sauce. The very small fruits resemble jelly beans.

Harold's St. Barts

Capsicum chinense 'Harold's St Barts'

ORIGIN Caribbean (St. Barts)

PODS 1.5–2.5 in. long, 1–1.5 in. wide; pendant, pale green to golden yellow

PLANT HEIGHT 24–30 in.

HARVEST Late season, 80–90 days after transplanting

HEAT LEVEL Very hot

Tasty, smoky flavor; used for chile powder and hot sauce.

Hot Paper Lantern

Capsicum chinense 'Hot Paper Lantern'

ORIGIN United States

PODS 3–4 in. long, 0.75–1.25 in. wide; pendant, green to orange to red

PLANT HEIGHT 18–24 in.

HARVEST Late season, 80–90 days after transplanting

HEAT LEVEL Very hot

A good variety for cool-season climates. Used for chile powder and hot sauce.

Jamaican Hot Chocolate

Capsicum chinense 'Jamaican Hot Chocolate'

ORIGIN Caribbean

PODS 2–2.5 in. long, 1.25–1.75 in. wide; pendant, dark green to reddish brown

PLANT HEIGHT 24–30 in.

HARVEST Very late season, 90 or more days after transplanting

HEAT LEVEL Extremely hot

Another brown *C. chinense* variety. Used for chile powder, hot sauce, and jerks and rubs.

Lantern

Capsicum chinense 'Lantern'

ORIGIN United States

PODS 1–1.5 in. long, 0.75–1 in. wide; pendant, green to bright orange

PLANT HEIGHT 18–24 in.

HARVEST Late season, 80–90 days after transplanting

HEAT LEVEL Very hot

Prolific. Shiny pointed fruits resemble toy tops. Used for chile powder and hot sauce.

Lester William's Red

Capsicum chinense 'Lester William's Red'

ORIGIN West Indies (St. Vincent)

PODS 1.5–1.75 in. long, 1–1.25 in. wide; pendant, pale green to orange to red

PLANT HEIGHT 18–24 in.

HARVEST Late season, 80–90 days after transplanting

HEAT LEVEL Hot

Collected during coauthor Janie's south Caribbean expedition. Used for chile powder and hot sauces.

Limon

Capsicum chinense 'Limon'

ORIGIN Peru

PODS 1.5–2 in. long, 0.5–0.625 in. wide; pendant, green to yellow

PLANT HEIGHT 12–18 in.

HARVEST Early season, 60–70 days after transplanting

HEAT LEVEL Very hot

An early habanero type; good for gardeners in cool-season climates. Prolific. Used for chile powder and hot sauce.

Malaysian Goronong

Capsicum chinense 'Malaysian Goronong'

ORIGIN Malaysia

PODS 2.5–3.5 in. long, 1.25–1.5 in. wide; pendant, pale green to yellow

PLANT HEIGHT 30–36 in.

HARVEST Very late season, 90 or more days after transplanting

HEAT LEVEL Very hot

Unusually shaped fruit. Used for chile powder and hot sauce.

Mayo Pimento

Capsicum chinense 'Mayo Pimento'

ORIGIN Unknown

PODS 2.75–3 in. long, 1–1.25 in. wide; pendant, green to orange to red

PLANT HEIGHT 18–24 in.

HARVEST Very late season, 90 or more days after transplanting

HEAT LEVEL Mild

Habanero flavor without the heat. Used as a seasoning pepper.

Moruga Scorpion

Capsicum chinense 'Moruga Scorpion'

ORIGIN Trinidad

PODS 2–2.5 in. long, 1.5–1.75 in. wide; pendant, green to orange to red

PLANT HEIGHT 24–30 in.

HARVEST Extremely late season, 120 or more days after transplanting

HEAT LEVEL Super hot

With a mean heat of 1.2 million SHUs, the New Mexico State University Chile Pepper Institute named this variety the hottest in the world in 2012–2013. Used for chile powder and hot sauce.

Moruga Scorpion Yellow

Capsicum chinense 'Moruga Scorpion Yellow'

ORIGIN Trinidad

PODS 2–2.5 in. long, 1.5–1.75 in. wide; pendant, green to yellow

PLANT HEIGHT 24–30 in.

HARVEST Extremely late season, 120 or more days after transplanting

HEAT LEVEL Extremely hot

The yellow version of 'Moruga Scorpion', but a bit milder. Used for chile powder and hot sauce.

Naga Morich

Capsicum chinense 'Naga Morich'

ORIGIN Bangladesh

PODS 1.5–2.5 in. long, 1–1.5 in. wide; pendant, green to orange to red

PLANT HEIGHT 18–24 in.

HARVEST Very late season, 90 or more days after transplanting

HEAT LEVEL Super hot

Related to 'Bhut Jolokia', although smaller pods mature earlier. Used for chile powder and hot sauce.

Orange Teapot

Capsicum chinense 'Orange Teapot'

ORIGIN Unknown

PODS 1.5–1.75 in. long, 0.375–0.5 in. wide; pendant, green to bright orange

PLANT HEIGHT 18–24 in.

HARVEST Very late season, 90 or more days after transplanting

HEAT LEVEL Very hot

Used for chile powder and hot sauce.

Peruvian Serlano

Capsicum chinense 'Peruvian Serlano'

ORIGIN Peru

PODS 1.75–2.5 in. long, 0.375–0.5 in. wide; pendant, green to red

PLANT HEIGHT 18–24 in.

HARVEST Very late season, 90 or more days after transplanting

HEAT LEVEL Very hot

Used for chile powder and hot sauce.

Pimiento de Chiero

Capsicum chinense 'Pimiento De Chiero'

ORIGIN South America

PODS 0.5–0.75 in. long, 0.25–0.375 in. wide; upright, green to yellow to creamy yellow

PLANT HEIGHT 18–24 in.

HARVEST Midseason, 70–80 days after transplanting

HEAT LEVEL Hot

Also known as 'Pimento do Cheiro'; the name translates to "aromatic pepper."

Puerto Rican No Burn

Capsicum chinense **'Puerto Rican No Burn'**

ORIGIN United States (Puerto Rico)

PODS 0.75–1 in. long and wide; upright to pendant, green to red

PLANT HEIGHT 18–24 in.

HARVEST Late season, 80–90 days after transplanting

HEAT LEVEL Sweet

Fantastic in Puerto Rican dishes; used as a seasoning pepper.

Regina's Hots

Capsicum chinense **'Regina's Hots'**

ORIGIN West Indies (St. Vincent)

PODS 2–2.5 in. long, 1–1.5 in. wide; pendant, green to orange to red

PLANT HEIGHT 18–24 in.

HARVEST Late season, 80–90 days after transplanting

HEAT LEVEL Very hot

Prolific. Named after Regina, who serenades shoppers while selling her chiles at the Kingstown Bay market in St. Vincent. Collected during coauthor Janie's south Caribbean expedition. Used for chile powder and hot sauce.

Rocotillo

Capsicum chinense **'Rocotillo'**

ORIGIN West Indies

PODS 1–1.5 in. long, 1–1.25 in. wide; pendant, green to red

PLANT HEIGHT 18–24 in.

HARVEST Late season, 80–90 days after transplanting

HEAT LEVEL Medium

This milder habanero is used as a seasoning pepper.

Scotch Bonnet Red

Capsicum chinense 'Scotch Bonnet Red'

ORIGIN Jamaica

PODS 1–1.5 in. long, 1–1.25 in. wide; pendant, green to orange to red

PLANT HEIGHT 18–24 in.

HARVEST Late season, 80–90 days after transplanting

HEAT LEVEL Very hot

This variety comes on a bit earlier than other habanero types. Used for chile powder, hot sauce, and jerk seasoning.

Scotch Bonnet Yellow

Capsicum chinense 'Scotch Bonnet Yellow'

ORIGIN Jamaica

PODS 1.5–2 in. long, 1.25–1.75 in. wide; pendant, green to yellow

PLANT HEIGHT 18–24 in.

HARVEST Very late season, 90 or more days after transplanting

HEAT LEVEL Very hot

Used for chile powder, hot sauce, and jerk seasoning.

Smokin' Ed's Carolina Reaper

Capsicum chinense 'Smokin' Ed's Carolina Reaper'

ORIGIN United States (South Carolina)

PODS 2–3 in. long, 1–1.5 in. wide; pendant, green to red

PLANT HEIGHT 30–36 in.

HARVEST Extremely late season, 120 or more days

HEAT LEVEL Super hot

In 2013 *Guinness World Records* listed this as the world's hottest pepper, peaking at 2.58 million SHUs. It is a protected plant variety developed by Ed Currie of Puckerbutt Pepper Company in South Carolina. Cross Country Nurseries is a licensed grower.

Tazmanian

Capsicum chinense 'Tazmanian'

ORIGIN Unknown

PODS 1.75–2 in. long, 1.25–1.5 in. wide; pendant, green to orange to red

PLANT HEIGHT 24–30 in.

HARVEST Very late season, 90 or more days after transplanting

HEAT LEVEL Very hot

Prolific. Used for chile powder and hot sauce. This pepper will take your breath away!

Tiger Teeth

Capsicum chinense 'Tiger Teeth'

ORIGIN Guyana

PODS 2–3 in. long, 0.75–1 in. wide; pendant, green to orange to red

PLANT HEIGHT 24–30 in.

HARVEST Late season, 80–90 days after transplanting

HEAT LEVEL Very hot

Used for chile powder and hot sauce.

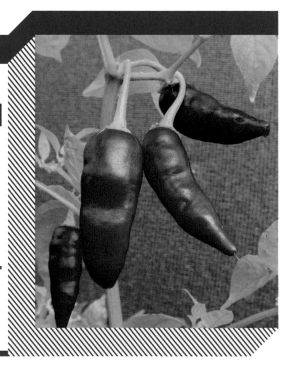

Tobago Seasoning

Capsicum chinense 'Tobago Seasoning'

ORIGIN Tobago

PODS 1.5–2.5 in. long, 0.75–1 in. wide; pendant, green to orange to red

PLANT HEIGHT 24–30 in.

HARVEST Late season, 80–90 days after transplanting

HEAT LEVEL Mild

Heirloom. Used as a seasoning pepper.

Trinidad Perfume

Capsicum chinense 'Trinidad Perfume'

ORIGIN Trinidad

PODS 1–1.5 in. long, 1–1.25 in. wide; pendant, green to bright yellow

PLANT HEIGHT 24–30 in.

HARVEST Late season, 80–90 days after transplanting

HEAT LEVEL Mild

Fantastic aroma and flavor with practically no heat; used as a seasoning pepper.

Trinidad Scorpion

Capsicum chinense 'Trinidad Scorpion'

ORIGIN Trinidad

PODS 2–2.5 in. long, 1.25–1.75 in. wide; pendant, green to orange to red

PLANT HEIGHT 24–30 in.

HARVEST Extremely late season, 120 or more days after transplanting

HEAT LEVEL Super hot

This is the Butch T strain. Peaking at 1.463 million SHUs, listed in *Guinness World Records* as the hottest pepper from 2011–2013. Used for chile powder and hot sauce.

Trinidad Seasoning

Capsicum chinense 'Trinidad Seasoning'

ORIGIN Trinidad

PODS 2.5–3 in. long, 0.75–1 in. wide; pendant, green to orange to red

PLANT HEIGHT 24–30 in.

HARVEST Very late season, 90 or more days after transplanting

HEAT LEVEL Mild

Fruity flavor with little heat; used as a seasoning pepper.

Trinidad Smooth

Capsicum chinense 'Trinidad Smooth'

ORIGIN Trinidad

PODS 1.25–1.75 in. long, 0.75–1 in. wide; pendant, green to orange to red

PLANT HEIGHT 24–30 in.

HARVEST Late season, 80–90 days after transplanting

HEAT LEVEL Mild

Found during coauthor Janie's south Caribbean expedition. Used as a seasoning pepper.

West Indian Red

Capsicum chinense 'West Indian Red'

ORIGIN Caribbean

PODS 1.5–2 in. long, 1–1.5 in. wide; pendant, green to red

PLANT HEIGHT 18–24 in.

HARVEST Late season, 80–90 days after transplanting

HEAT LEVEL Very hot

Developed by CARDI (Caribbean Agricultural Research and Development Institute) in Antigua and Barbuda. Used for chile powder and hot sauce.

Wild Brazil

Capsicum chinense 'Wild Brazil'

ORIGIN Brazil

PODS 0.25–0.375 in. long, 0.25to 0.375 in. wide; upright, green to yellow to pale yellow

PLANT HEIGHT 18–24 in.

HARVEST Late season, 80–90 days after transplanting

HEAT LEVEL Very hot

A wild cultivar. Used for chile powder.

Wiri Wiri

Capsicum chinense 'Wiri Wiri'

ORIGIN Guyana

PODS 0. 25–0.375 in. long, 0.25–0.375 in. wide; upright, green to red

PLANT HEIGHT 24–30 in.

HARVEST Late season, 80–90 days after transplanting

HEAT LEVEL Hot

Sometimes listed as a cultivar of *C. frutescens*. Used to make Guyanese pepper sauce.

Yellow Sun

Capsicum chinense 'Yellow Sun'

ORIGIN Unknown

PODS 2–2.5 in. long, 1.5–2 in. wide; pendant, green to bright yellow

PLANT HEIGHT 24–30 in.

HARVEST Late season, 80–90 days after transplanting

HEAT LEVEL Very hot

Used for chile powder and hot sauce.

Yuquitania

Capsicum chinense 'Yuquitania'

ORIGIN Mexico

PODS 1.25–1.5 in. long, 0.375–0.5 in. wide; pendant, pale green to orange to red

PLANT HEIGHT 18–24 in.

HARVEST Late season, 80–90 days after transplanting

HEAT LEVEL Very hot

Pods are tear-shaped. Used to make hot sauce.

Capsicum frutescens

The tabasco chile is the best-known variety of this species, being the primary ingredient in the famous sauce that is now more than 125 years old. Another famous variety is 'Malagueta', which grows wild in the Amazon basin in Brazil, where the species probably originated.

Curiously, there are not as many names for the wild varieties as there are with some other species, but the most common is "bird pepper." No domesticated *C. frutescens* has ever been found in an archaeological site in Middle or South America, but ethno-botanists speculate that the domestication site was probably in Panama and from there it spread to Mexico and the Caribbean.

At any rate, we know the tabasco variety of *C. frutescens* was being cultivated near Tabasco, Mexico, in the early 1840s because it was transferred to Louisiana in 1848, where it was eventually grown to produce Tabasco sauce. Demand outstripped supply, and today tabascos are commercially grown in Central America and Colombia and shipped in mash form to Louisiana. Tabasco peppers in Louisiana fell victim to the tobacco etch virus, but were rescued in 1970 with the introduction of 'Tabasco Green-leaf', a TEV-resistant variety. Today at Avery Island, the site of the original Tabasco growing and manufacturing operation, there are still fields of tabascos under cultivation, but they are mostly for crop improvement and seed production.

Some varieties of *C. frutescens* found their way to Africa, India, and East Asia, where they are still called bird peppers, and cultivated to make hot sauce and curries. *Capsicum frutescens* plants have a compact habit, an intermediate number of stems, and grow between 1 and 4 feet high, depending on climate and growing conditions. The leaves are ovate and smooth. The flowers have greenish white corollas with no spots and purple anthers. The pods are borne erect and measure up to 1½ inches long and ⅜ inch wide. Immature pods are yellow or green, maturing to bright red. The peppers are quite hot, measuring between 30,000 and 50,000 SHUs.

The height of the plants depends on climate, with plants growing the largest in warmer areas. The plant is particularly good for container gardening, and one of our specimens lived as a perennial for four years in a pot, but gradually lost vigor and produced fewer pods each year.

Capsicum frutescens and *C. pubescens* have fewer pod shapes, sizes, and colors than *C. annuum*, *C. chinense*, and *C. baccatum*, though no one knows why this is. It is important to remember that the diversity of pod morphology is human-guided; in other words, the differences one sees in pod size and shape are because humans conscientiously made choices on which pods to save for the next growing season. In nature, wild chile plants usually have small, erect red fruits that drop off easily. The small fruit and easy fruit drop traits are beneficial for bird dispersal. However, humans prefer large fruit and fruit that stays attached to the plant until harvested. Thus, under domestication these traits are modified.

Capsicum frutescens has small fruit that drops off easily. Therefore, an explanation for the lack of fruit shapes in the species is that it is still mostly a wild form. It is found growing in the same areas as *C. annuum* and *C. chinense*, so selection may have been on *C. annuum* and *C. chinense*, while *C. frutescens* had little or no selection.

The most common use for the pods is for hot sauce; they are crushed, salted, fermented, and combined with vinegar. However, the pods can be used fresh in salsas and can be dried for use in stir-fries.

Angkor Sunrise

Capsicum frutescens 'Angkor Sunrise'

ORIGIN Cambodia

PODS 1–1.5 in. long, 0.375–0.5 in. wide; upright, pale yellow to orange to red

PLANT HEIGHT 42–48 in.

HARVEST Very late season, 90 or more days after transplanting

HEAT LEVEL Very hot

Prolific; relative of tabasco. The seed was originally collected in Cambodia and named by food and travel writer Richard Sterling and sent to coauthor Dave, who dispersed the seeds to collectors.

Del Diablo

Capsicum frutescens 'Del Diablo'

ORIGIN Oaxaca, Mexico

PODS 0.5–0.625 in. long, 0.25–0.375 in. wide; upright, green to red

PLANT HEIGHT 30–36 in.

HARVEST Very late season, 90 or more days after transplanting

HEAT LEVEL Extremely hot

Prolific. Used dried in Mexican cuisine and in sauces.

Guam Boonies

Capsicum frutescens 'Guam Boonies'

ORIGIN Guam

PODS 1–1.25 in. long, 0.5–0.75 in. wide; upright, green to orange to red

PLANT HEIGHT 36–42 in.

HARVEST Very late season, 90 or more days after transplanting

HEAT LEVEL Very hot

Used for chile powder and sauces.

Hawaiian Red Kona

Capsicum frutescens 'Hawaiian Red Kona'

ORIGIN United States (Hawaii)

PODS 0.75 to1.25 in. long, 0.25–0.375 in. wide; upright, pale green to orange to red

PLANT HEIGHT 36–42 in.

HARVEST Very late season, 90 or more days after transplanting

HEAT LEVEL Very hot

Used for chile powder and hot sauce.

Malagueta

Capsicum frutescens 'Malagueta'

ORIGIN Brazil

PODS 1 to1.25 in. long, 0.375–0.5 in. wide; upright, green to red

PLANT HEIGHT 30–36 in.

HARVEST Very late season, 90 or more days after transplanting

HEAT LEVEL Very hot

A relative of tabasco also known as 'Piri Piri' in Portugal and Mozambique. Used for chile powder and hot sauce.

Pilli Pilli

Capsicum frutescens 'Pilli Pilli'

ORIGIN Africa

PODS 0.5–0.75 in. long, 0.25–0.375 in. long; upright, green to red

PLANT HEIGHT 24–30 in.

HARVEST Very late season, 90 or more days after transplanting

HEAT LEVEL Very hot

Also known as 'Piri Piri' and 'Pili Pili'. Used for chile powder and hot sauce.

Siling Labuyo

Capsicum frutescens 'Siling Labuyo'

ORIGIN Philippines

PODS 1–1.5 in. long, 0.25–0.375 in. wide; upright, green to red

PLANT HEIGHT 36–42 in.

HARVEST Very late season, 90 or more days after transplanting

HEAT LEVEL Very hot

Used for chile powder and hot sauce.

Tabasco

Capsicum frutescens 'Tabasco'

ORIGIN United States (Louisiana)

PODS 1–1.5 in. long, 0.25–0.375 in. wide; upright, yellow to orange to red

PLANT HEIGHT 36–42 in.

HARVEST Very late season, 90 or more days after transplanting

HEAT LEVEL Very hot

Prolific. Used for chile powder and hot sauce.

Tabasco Greenleaf

Capsicum frutescens 'Tabasco Greenleaf'

ORIGIN United States

PODS 1–1.25 in. long, 0.25–0.375 in. wide; upright, greenish yellow to yellow to orange to red

PLANT HEIGHT 24–30 in.

HARVEST Very late season, 90 or more days after transplanting

HEAT LEVEL Very hot

Prolific and disease resistant. Used for chile powder and hot sauce.

Zimbabwe Bird

Capsicum frutescens 'Zimbabwe Bird'

ORIGIN Africa

PODS 0.75–1 in. long, 0.375–0.5 in. wide; upright, green to orange to red

PLANT HEIGHT 30–36 in.

HARVEST Very late season, 90 or more days after transplanting

HEAT LEVEL Very hot

Used dried and crushed on meats, soups, and stews.

Capsicum pubescens

Capsicum pubescens is the only domesticated *Capsicum* species with no wild form; however, two wild species, *C. cardenasii* and *C. eximium*, are closely related.

The center of origin for this species was Bolivia, and the species was probably domesticated about 6000 BC, making it one of the oldest domesticated plants in the Americas. Botanist Charles Heiser, citing Garcilaso de la Vega (1609), notes that *C. pubescens* was "the most common pepper among the Incas, just as it is today in Cuzco, the former capital of the Incan empire."

It is grown today in the Andes from Chile to Colombia, mostly in small family plots. It is also cultivated in highland areas of Central America and Mexico. The common name for this species in South America is rocoto or locoto. In Mexico, it is also called *chile manzano* (apple pepper), and *chile perón* (pear pepper), names that call attention to the fruitlike shapes of the peppers. In some parts of Mexico and Guatemala, they use the name *chile caballo*, or horse pepper. Yellow *C. pubescens* are called *canarios*, or canaries, in parts of Mexico, particularly Oaxaca.

It has a compact to erect habit (sometimes sprawling and vinelike) and grows up to 4 feet tall, but 2 feet is more typical in US gardens. In Bolivia, they grow to 15 feet. The leaves are ovate, light to dark green, very pubescent (hairy).

The flowers have purple corollas, purple and white anthers, and stand erect above the leaves. The pods are round, sometimes pear-shaped, measuring about 2–3 inches long and 2–2½ inches wide, but pods as large as bell peppers have been reported. The pods are green in their immature state, maturing to yellow, orange, or red.

Their heat level is 30,000–50,000 SHUs and higher. *Capsicum pubescens* varieties contain a unique set of capsaicinoids (pungency compounds), causing some people to believe they are hotter than habaneros. In parts of the Americas they are referred to as "el mas picante de los picantes," the hottest of the hot.

As with *C. frutescens*, there is a lack of pod diversity within the species. The fruits are large and stay attached to the plant. While there are wild forms of *C. annuum*, *C. chinense*, and *C.*

baccatum, no *C. pubescens* plant has ever been found with small fruits that easily separate from the plant. It has been suggested that *C. pubescens* was domesticated so long ago that its wild form is extinct. But why is the variability less? One explanation is that when *C. pubescens* was domesticated it went through a "founders effect," which is when the establishment of a new population is founded by a few original individuals that carry only a small fraction of the total genetic variation of the parental population. If this was the case, there is not enough genetic diversity to allow for genetic recombination to produce the assortment of pod forms seen in the other species. Furthermore, *C. pubescens* is isolated from other domesticated species and so cannot cross-pollinate with them, thereby reducing the available genes. Another factor may be the climate it grows best in; because it thrives only in a narrow temperature range, it may not have been grown in as many places, thus reducing the opportunity for selection by humans.

Scientists are presently addressing this question with sophisticated molecular techniques, and their work may shed further light on the lack of pod diversity within a few years. Of course, this all depends on having the genetic resources available—the seeds of the future.

Capsicum pubescens plants are traditionally grown in high mountain areas of tropical countries. They can survive very light frosts but not hard freezes. Some sources state that because of their long growing season and need for longer days, *C. pubescens* varieties are unsuitable for cultivation in the United States. However, our experiments have shown that plants started early can achieve fruiting within one season. The species also responds well to shading because the foliage has a tendency to burn in full sun. The growing season is long, 120 days or more after transplanting.

Because it is adapted to the cooler highland temperatures, *C. pubescens* grows best under cooler conditions. This can be under a cool coastal climate, a mountain garden, or in an artificial climate, such as a cooled greenhouse. The plants can live for several years in a pot. Coauthor Dave kept two rocoto plants in separate pots growing for eight years, but their vigor diminished over time.

Capsicum pubescens varieties are usually consumed in their fresh form because the pods are difficult to dry out as a result of their thickness. They are commonly used in fresh salsas, and the larger pods can be stuffed with meat or cheese and baked.

Rocoto Red

Capsicum pubescens 'Rocoto Red'

ORIGIN Andes

PODS 1.5–2 in. long, 1.25–1.5 in. wide; pendant, green to red

PLANT HEIGHT 48 in. (or more)

HARVEST Extremely late season, 120 or more days after transplanting

HEAT LEVEL Very hot

Also known as 'Manzano'. Used fresh in salsas; larger pods can be stuffed and baked.

Rocoto Yellow

Capsicum pubescens 'Rocoto Yellow'

ORIGIN Andes

PODS 1.5–2 in. long, 1.25–1.5 in. wide; pendant, green to yellow

PLANT HEIGHT 48 in. (or more)

HARVEST Extremely late season, 120 or more days after transplanting

HEAT LEVEL Very hot

Also known as 'Canario'. Used fresh in salsas; larger pods can be stuffed and baked.

Conversion Tables

TEMPERATURES

°C = 5/9 × (°F–32)

°F = (9/5 × °C) + 32

MEASUREMENTS

INCHES	CENTIMETERS		FEET	METERS
0.5	1.3		1	0.3
1	2.5		2	0.6
2	5.1		3	0.9
3	7.6		4	1.2
4	10		5	1.5
5	13		6	1.8
6	15		7	2.1
7	18		8	2.4
8	20		9	2.7
9	23		10	3.0
10	25		12	3.6
12	30		15	4.5
18	46		20	6.0
20	51		25	7.5
24	61		30	9.0
30	76			

Seed Company Sources

Be aware that there are often many sources for seeds, so use the Internet to search for each and every variety you're interested in. In this list below, we've only included sources that we've generally had good luck with. Keep in mind, however, that when purchasing seed you're always taking a small risk. There's no guarantee that what you received one year will be what you receive in the next.

For live plants, all of the varieties we discuss in the book are available from coauthor Janie's Cross Country Nurseries in New Jersey, or at ChilePlants.com.

123 Seeds
Ritthemsestraat 13
4388 JM Oost-Souhurg
The Netherlands
123Seeds.com

**Baker Creek Heirloom
Seed Co.**
2278 Baker Creek Road
Mansfield, MO 65704
RareSeeds.com

Buckeye Pepper Co.
1475 Lutz Road
Lima, OH 45801
BuckeyePepper.com

Burpee Seed
300 Park Avenue
Warminster, PA 18974
Burpee.com

Chile Pepper Institute
New Mexico State University
113 West University Ave
Las Cruces, NM 88003
ChilePepperInstitute.org

Cross Country Nurseries
PO Box 170
199 Kingwood-Locktown Road
Rosemont, NJ 08556
ChilePlants.com

Evergreen Seeds
P.O. Box 17538
Anaheim, CA 92817
EvergreenSeeds.com

Fedco Seeds
P.O. Box 520
Waterville, ME 04903
FedcoSeeds.com

Fords Fiery Foods
Eugene, OR
FordsFieryFoodsandPlants.com

Grow Italian
P.O. Box 3908
Lawrence, KS 66046
GrowItalian.com

Harris Seeds
355 Paul Road
P.O. Box 24966
Rochester, NY 14624-0966
HarrisSeeds.com

Hippy Seed Co.
P.O. Box 410
Ettalong Beach
NSW 2257
Australia
TheHippySeedCompany.com

HPS Seeds
334 W. Stroud Street, Ste. #1
Randolph, WI 53956-1341
HPSSeed.com

Irish Eyes Garden Seeds
5045 Robinson Canyon Road
Ellensburg, WA 98926
IrishEyesGardenSeeds.com

Johnny's Selected Seeds
13 Main Street
Fairfield, ME 04937
Johnnyseeds.com

Kitchen Garden Seeds
23 Tulip Drive
P.O. Box 638
Bantam, CT 06750
KitchenGardenSeeds.com

Kitazawa Seed Company
201 4th Street, #206
Oakland, CA 94607
KitazawaSeed.com

Lake Valley Seeds
5717 Arapahoe Ave
Boulder, CO 80303
LakeValleySeed.com

Local Harvest
P.O. Box 1292
Santa Cruz, CA 95061
LocalHarvest.org

Native Seeds/SEARCH
3061 N. Campbell Avenue
Tucson, AZ 85719
NativeSeeds.org

Park Seed
3507 Cokesbury Road
Hodges, SC 29653
ParkSeed.com

Pepper Joe's
725 Carolina Farm Blvd
Myrtle Beach, SC 29579
PepperJoe.com

Pepper Lover
PepperLover.com

Puckerbutt Pepper Company
235 Main Street
Fort Mill, SC 29715
PuckerbuttPepperCompany.com

Redwood Seeds
P.O. Box 431
Manton, CA 96059
RedwoodSeeds.net

Refining Fire Chiles
13409 Bubbling Lane
Lakeside, CA 92040
SuperHotChiles.com

Sandia Seed Company
P.O. Box 20211
Albuquerque, NM 87154
SandiaSeed.com

Seed Savers Exchange
3094 North Winn Road
Decorah, IA 52101
SeedSavers.org

Seedman
Seedman.com

Seeds of Change
P.O. Box 4908
Rancho Dominguez, CA 90220
SeedsofChange.com

Seeds by Design
P.O. Box 602
4599 McDermott Road
Maxwell, CA 95955
SeedsbyDesign.com

Seeds from Italy
GrowItalian.com

Sieger's Seed Company
13031 Reflections Drive
Holland, MI 49424
Siegers.com

Siskiyou Seeds
3220 East Fork Road
Williams, OR 97544
SiskiyouSeeds.com

Southern Exposure Seed Exchange
P.O. Box 460
Mineral, VA 23117
SouthernExposure.com

Stokes Seeds
P.O. Box 548
Buffalo, NY 14240-0548
StokesSeeds.com

Territorial Seeds
P.O. Box 158
Cottage Grove, OR 97424
TerritorialSeed.com

Tomato Growers Supply
P.O. Box 60015
Fort Myers, FL 33906
TomatoGrowers.com

Tradewinds Fruit
P.O. Box 9396
Santa Rosa, CA 95405
TradewindsFruit.com

Index

Dave DeWitt

Dave DeWitt has written and coauthored more than 30 books on peppers. Formerly chair of the board of the New Mexico Farm and Ranch Heritage Museum, Dave is an adjunct professor at New Mexico State University. His media company, Sunbelt Shows, Inc., produces the annual National Fiery Foods & Barbecue Show.

Janie

Janie Lamson
Nurseries in
growing pepp
ChilePlants.co
peppers, ship
chiles through
many years o
along with he
has provided
the world of